FRACTION
MATH
WORKBOOK

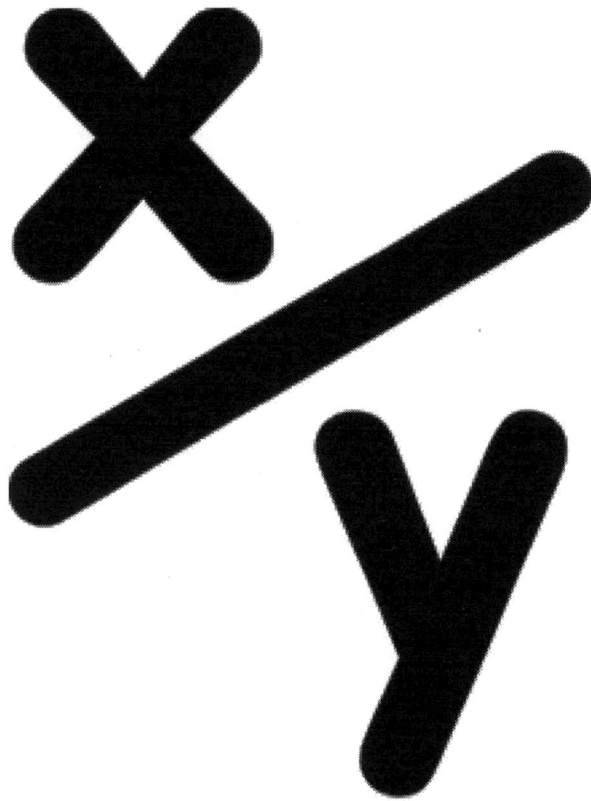

EXERCISES 1

FRACTIONS ADDITION

1. $\dfrac{2}{3} + \dfrac{2}{3} =$ ....

2. $\dfrac{2}{5} + \dfrac{4}{5} =$ ....

3. $\dfrac{3}{5} + \dfrac{4}{5} =$ ....

4. $\dfrac{3}{4} + \dfrac{1}{4} =$ ....

5. $\dfrac{1}{2} + \dfrac{1}{2} =$ ....

6. $\dfrac{1}{6} + \dfrac{1}{6} =$ ....

7. $\dfrac{3}{10} + \dfrac{4}{10} =$ ....

8. $\dfrac{1}{3} + \dfrac{2}{3} =$ ....

9. $\dfrac{9}{10} + \dfrac{3}{10} =$ ....

10. $\dfrac{3}{6} + \dfrac{4}{6} =$ ....

11. $\dfrac{1}{4} + \dfrac{1}{4} =$ ....

12. $\dfrac{7}{10} + \dfrac{6}{10} =$ ....

13. $\dfrac{3}{5} + \dfrac{2}{5} =$ ....

14. $\dfrac{2}{6} + \dfrac{3}{6} =$ ....

15. $\dfrac{1}{6} + \dfrac{4}{6} =$ ....

16. $\dfrac{4}{10} + \dfrac{4}{10} =$ ....

17. $\dfrac{1}{4} + \dfrac{3}{4} =$ ....

18. $\dfrac{4}{5} + \dfrac{4}{5} =$ ....

19. $\dfrac{4}{10} + \dfrac{6}{10} =$ ....

20. $\dfrac{2}{3} + \dfrac{1}{3} =$ ....

21. $\dfrac{3}{10} + \dfrac{7}{10} =$ ....

22. $\dfrac{4}{5} + \dfrac{2}{5} =$ ....

23. $\dfrac{5}{6} + \dfrac{3}{6} =$ ....

24. $\dfrac{3}{4} + \dfrac{2}{4} =$ ....

25. $\dfrac{2}{10} + \dfrac{7}{10} =$ ....

26. $\dfrac{2}{4} + \dfrac{3}{4} =$ ....

27. $\dfrac{6}{10} + \dfrac{8}{10} =$ ....

28. $\dfrac{2}{6} + \dfrac{5}{6} =$ ....

29. $\dfrac{2}{4} + \dfrac{2}{4} =$ ....

30. $\dfrac{1}{5} + \dfrac{1}{5} =$ ....

31. $\dfrac{9}{10} + \dfrac{5}{10} =$ ....

32. $\dfrac{5}{6} + \dfrac{2}{6} =$ ....

33. $\dfrac{1}{3} + \dfrac{1}{3} =$ ....

34. $\dfrac{4}{6} + \dfrac{4}{6} =$ ....

35. $\dfrac{6}{10} + \dfrac{1}{10} =$ ....

36. $\dfrac{4}{5} + \dfrac{3}{5} =$ ....

37. $\dfrac{1}{6} + \dfrac{3}{6} =$ ....

38. $\dfrac{1}{10} + \dfrac{3}{10} =$ ....

39. $\dfrac{8}{10} + \dfrac{7}{10} =$ ....

40. $\dfrac{6}{10} + \dfrac{2}{10} =$ ....

41. $\dfrac{3}{5} + \dfrac{3}{5} =$ ....

42. $\dfrac{1}{6} + \dfrac{5}{6} =$ ....

43. $\dfrac{2}{4} + \dfrac{1}{4} =$ ....

44. $\dfrac{6}{10} + \dfrac{5}{10} =$ ....

45. $\dfrac{4}{6} + \dfrac{3}{6} =$ ....

46. $\dfrac{7}{10} + \dfrac{2}{10} =$ ....

47. $\dfrac{2}{5} + \dfrac{1}{5} =$ ....

48. $\dfrac{2}{6} + \dfrac{1}{6} =$ ....

49. $\dfrac{1}{5} + \dfrac{3}{5} =$

50. $\dfrac{1}{4} + \dfrac{2}{4} =$

51. $\dfrac{4}{6} + \dfrac{5}{6} =$

52. $\dfrac{4}{10} + \dfrac{8}{10} =$

53. $\dfrac{3}{10} + \dfrac{6}{10} =$

54. $\dfrac{2}{6} + \dfrac{2}{6} =$

55. $\dfrac{3}{4} + \dfrac{3}{4} =$

56. $\dfrac{2}{5} + \dfrac{3}{5} =$

57. $\dfrac{9}{10} + \dfrac{8}{10} =$

58. $\dfrac{5}{6} + \dfrac{4}{6} =$

59. $\dfrac{8}{10} + \dfrac{6}{10} =$

60. $\dfrac{6}{10} + \dfrac{6}{10} =$

61. $\dfrac{8}{10} + \dfrac{3}{10} =$

62. $\dfrac{8}{10} + \dfrac{9}{10} =$

63. $\dfrac{2}{10} + \dfrac{8}{10} =$

64. $\dfrac{1}{6} + \dfrac{2}{6} =$

65. $\dfrac{5}{10} + \dfrac{9}{10} =$ ....

66. $\dfrac{3}{6} + \dfrac{1}{6} =$ ....

67. $\dfrac{8}{10} + \dfrac{5}{10} =$ ....

68. $\dfrac{2}{10} + \dfrac{5}{10} =$ ....

69. $\dfrac{7}{10} + \dfrac{8}{10} =$ ....

70. $\dfrac{3}{6} + \dfrac{2}{6} =$ ....

71. $\dfrac{4}{5} + \dfrac{1}{5} =$ ....

72. $\dfrac{8}{10} + \dfrac{4}{10} =$ ....

73. $\dfrac{5}{6} + \dfrac{1}{6} =$ ....

74. $\dfrac{2}{5} + \dfrac{2}{5} =$ ....

75. $\dfrac{1}{10} + \dfrac{6}{10} =$ ....

76. $\dfrac{5}{6} + \dfrac{5}{6} =$ ....

77. $\dfrac{3}{6} + \dfrac{3}{6} =$ ....

78. $\dfrac{9}{10} + \dfrac{9}{10} =$ ....

79. $\dfrac{4}{10} + \dfrac{9}{10} =$ ....

80. $\dfrac{1}{5} + \dfrac{2}{5} =$ ....

81. $\dfrac{5}{10} + \dfrac{5}{10} =$ ....

82. $\dfrac{5}{10} + \dfrac{6}{10} =$ ....

83. $\dfrac{5}{10} + \dfrac{2}{10} =$ ....

84. $\dfrac{4}{6} + \dfrac{1}{6} =$ ....

85. $\dfrac{1}{5} + \dfrac{4}{5} =$ ....

86. $\dfrac{1}{10} + \dfrac{9}{10} =$ ....

87. $\dfrac{2}{10} + \dfrac{3}{10} =$ ....

88. $\dfrac{9}{10} + \dfrac{6}{10} =$ ....

89. $\dfrac{3}{10} + \dfrac{3}{10} =$ ....

90. $\dfrac{3}{5} + \dfrac{1}{5} =$ ....

91. $\dfrac{4}{10} + \dfrac{1}{10} =$ ....

92. $\dfrac{1}{10} + \dfrac{8}{10} =$ ....

93. $\dfrac{1}{10} + \dfrac{2}{10} =$ ....

94. $\dfrac{3}{10} + \dfrac{9}{10} =$ ....

95. $\dfrac{7}{10} + \dfrac{1}{10} =$ ....

96. $\dfrac{2}{10} + \dfrac{2}{10} =$ ....

97. $\dfrac{5}{12} + \dfrac{8}{12} =$ ....

98. $\dfrac{7}{13} + \dfrac{6}{13} =$ ....

99. $\dfrac{3}{7} + \dfrac{4}{7} =$ ....

100. $\dfrac{8}{16} + \dfrac{8}{16} =$ ....

101. $\dfrac{3}{8} + \dfrac{1}{8} =$ ....

102. $\dfrac{3}{11} + \dfrac{1}{11} =$ ....

103. $\dfrac{9}{14} + \dfrac{2}{14} =$ ....

104. $\dfrac{7}{9} + \dfrac{4}{9} =$ ....

105. $\dfrac{7}{13} + \dfrac{3}{13} =$ ....

106. $\dfrac{6}{15} + \dfrac{5}{15} =$ ....

107. $\dfrac{7}{12} + \dfrac{11}{12} =$ ....

108. $\dfrac{5}{11} + \dfrac{8}{11} =$ ....

109. $\dfrac{11}{12} + \dfrac{10}{12} =$ ....

110. $\dfrac{5}{9} + \dfrac{5}{9} =$ ....

111. $\dfrac{10}{13} + \dfrac{6}{13} =$ ....

112. $\dfrac{1}{15} + \dfrac{10}{15} =$ ....

113. $\dfrac{12}{14} + \dfrac{8}{14} =$ ....

114. $\dfrac{1}{16} + \dfrac{8}{16} =$ ....

115. $\dfrac{1}{7} + \dfrac{5}{7} =$ ....

116. $\dfrac{7}{8} + \dfrac{6}{8} =$ ....

117. $\dfrac{2}{11} + \dfrac{10}{11} =$ ....

118. $\dfrac{2}{9} + \dfrac{7}{9} =$ ....

119. $\dfrac{7}{8} + \dfrac{7}{8} =$ ....

120. $\dfrac{2}{14} + \dfrac{6}{14} =$ ....

121. $\dfrac{6}{15} + \dfrac{6}{15} =$ ....

122. $\dfrac{3}{12} + \dfrac{3}{12} =$ ....

123. $\dfrac{10}{13} + \dfrac{5}{13} =$ ....

124. $\dfrac{1}{7} + \dfrac{3}{7} =$ ....

125. $\dfrac{5}{16} + \dfrac{12}{16} =$ ....

126. $\dfrac{4}{8} + \dfrac{5}{8} =$ ....

127. $\dfrac{15}{16} + \dfrac{15}{16} =$ ....

128. $\dfrac{6}{9} + \dfrac{7}{9} =$ ....

129. $\dfrac{2}{12} + \dfrac{6}{12} =$ ....

130. $\dfrac{3}{13} + \dfrac{1}{13} =$ ....

131. $\dfrac{1}{7} + \dfrac{2}{7} =$ ....

132. $\dfrac{6}{14} + \dfrac{12}{14} =$ ....

133. $\dfrac{4}{15} + \dfrac{9}{15} =$ ....

134. $\dfrac{2}{11} + \dfrac{6}{11} =$ ....

135. $\dfrac{12}{16} + \dfrac{9}{16} =$ ....

136. $\dfrac{7}{8} + \dfrac{1}{8} =$ ....

137. $\dfrac{5}{7} + \dfrac{2}{7} =$ ....

138. $\dfrac{3}{11} + \dfrac{4}{11} =$ ....

139. $\dfrac{3}{15} + \dfrac{12}{15} =$ ....

140. $\dfrac{8}{9} + \dfrac{4}{9} =$ ....

141. $\dfrac{7}{13} + \dfrac{7}{13} =$ ....

142. $\dfrac{2}{14} + \dfrac{5}{14} =$ ....

143. $\dfrac{5}{7} + \dfrac{1}{7} =$ ....

144. $\dfrac{4}{15} + \dfrac{4}{15} =$ ....

145. $\dfrac{8}{11} + \dfrac{4}{11} =$ ....

146. $\dfrac{6}{9} + \dfrac{1}{9} =$ ....

147. $\dfrac{5}{14} + \dfrac{1}{14} =$ ....

148. $\dfrac{1}{13} + \dfrac{5}{13} =$ ....

149. $\dfrac{7}{8} + \dfrac{2}{8} =$ ....

150. $\dfrac{4}{16} + \dfrac{8}{16} =$ ....

151. $\dfrac{8}{12} + \dfrac{9}{12} =$ ....

152. $\dfrac{13}{15} + \dfrac{8}{15} =$ ....

153. $\dfrac{11}{12} + \dfrac{9}{12} =$ ....

154. $\dfrac{6}{8} + \dfrac{3}{8} =$ ....

155. $\dfrac{9}{14} + \dfrac{4}{14} =$ ....

156. $\dfrac{8}{13} + \dfrac{9}{13} =$ ....

157. $\dfrac{6}{11} + \dfrac{6}{11} =$ ....

158. $\dfrac{2}{16} + \dfrac{3}{16} =$ ....

159. $\dfrac{5}{7} + \dfrac{6}{7} =$ ....

160. $\dfrac{7}{9} + \dfrac{1}{9} =$ ....

161. $\dfrac{6}{16} + \dfrac{10}{16} =$ ....

162. $\dfrac{11}{13} + \dfrac{2}{13} =$ ....

163. $\dfrac{5}{15} + \dfrac{12}{15} =$ ....

164. $\dfrac{6}{7} + \dfrac{5}{7} =$ ....

165. $\dfrac{11}{14} + \dfrac{6}{14} =$ ....

166. $\dfrac{3}{8} + \dfrac{5}{8} =$ ....

167. $\dfrac{5}{12} + \dfrac{1}{12} =$ ....

168. $\dfrac{7}{15} + \dfrac{12}{15} =$ ....

169. $\dfrac{9}{14} + \dfrac{7}{14} =$ ....

170. $\dfrac{12}{16} + \dfrac{14}{16} =$ ....

171. $\dfrac{4}{7} + \dfrac{5}{7} =$ ....

172. $\dfrac{10}{11} + \dfrac{9}{11} =$ ....

173. $\dfrac{5}{8} + \dfrac{1}{8} =$ ....

174. $\dfrac{6}{13} + \dfrac{3}{13} =$ ....

175. $\dfrac{2}{9} + \dfrac{2}{9} =$ ....

176. $\dfrac{11}{12} + \dfrac{5}{12} =$ ....

177. $\dfrac{2}{15} + \dfrac{5}{15} =$

178. $\dfrac{8}{9} + \dfrac{5}{9} =$

179. $\dfrac{1}{8} + \dfrac{6}{8} =$

180. $\dfrac{5}{13} + \dfrac{12}{13} =$

181. $\dfrac{6}{12} + \dfrac{6}{12} =$

182. $\dfrac{5}{7} + \dfrac{5}{7} =$

183. $\dfrac{9}{11} + \dfrac{2}{11} =$

184. $\dfrac{6}{14} + \dfrac{9}{14} =$

185. $\dfrac{9}{16} + \dfrac{8}{16} =$

186. $\dfrac{11}{13} + \dfrac{4}{13} =$

187. $\dfrac{8}{11} + \dfrac{5}{11} =$

188. $\dfrac{2}{14} + \dfrac{1}{14} =$

189. $\dfrac{3}{16} + \dfrac{8}{16} =$

190. $\dfrac{2}{8} + \dfrac{6}{8} =$

191. $\dfrac{3}{15} + \dfrac{2}{15} =$

192. $\dfrac{6}{7} + \dfrac{4}{7} =$

193. $\dfrac{5}{6} + \dfrac{2}{5} =$

194. $\dfrac{4}{8} + \dfrac{2}{3} =$

195. $\dfrac{2}{10} + \dfrac{3}{8} =$

196. $\dfrac{4}{6} + \dfrac{3}{4} =$

197. $\dfrac{3}{8} + \dfrac{3}{6} =$

198. $\dfrac{1}{2} + \dfrac{2}{5} =$

199. $\dfrac{5}{6} + \dfrac{4}{5} =$

200. $\dfrac{2}{4} + \dfrac{3}{8} =$

201. $\dfrac{9}{10} + \dfrac{6}{8} =$

202. $\dfrac{5}{6} + \dfrac{4}{6} =$

203. $\dfrac{7}{10} + \dfrac{1}{4} =$

204. $\dfrac{3}{4} + \dfrac{2}{4} =$

205. $\dfrac{6}{10} + \dfrac{2}{8} =$

206. $\dfrac{5}{6} + \dfrac{1}{3} =$

207. $\dfrac{1}{2} + \dfrac{1}{6} =$

208. $\dfrac{4}{6} + \dfrac{6}{8} =$

209. $\dfrac{1}{6} + \dfrac{2}{4} =$ ....

210. $\dfrac{3}{4} + \dfrac{1}{3} =$ ....

211. $\dfrac{2}{4} + \dfrac{2}{8} =$ ....

212. $\dfrac{1}{2} + \dfrac{3}{4} =$ ....

213. $\dfrac{2}{10} + \dfrac{5}{8} =$ ....

214. $\dfrac{1}{4} + \dfrac{1}{5} =$ ....

215. $\dfrac{1}{10} + \dfrac{4}{6} =$ ....

216. $\dfrac{1}{4} + \dfrac{5}{8} =$ ....

217. $\dfrac{1}{10} + \dfrac{2}{3} =$ ....

218. $\dfrac{1}{2} + \dfrac{4}{5} =$ ....

219. $\dfrac{3}{10} + \dfrac{1}{8} =$ ....

220. $\dfrac{5}{8} + \dfrac{2}{6} =$ ....

221. $\dfrac{1}{4} + \dfrac{2}{4} =$ ....

222. $\dfrac{4}{6} + \dfrac{1}{5} =$ ....

223. $\dfrac{4}{6} + \dfrac{3}{6} =$ ....

224. $\dfrac{7}{10} + \dfrac{3}{8} =$ ....

225. $\dfrac{3}{8} + \dfrac{1}{3} =$

226. $\dfrac{1}{6} + \dfrac{2}{6} =$

227. $\dfrac{8}{10} + \dfrac{3}{4} =$

228. $\dfrac{3}{8} + \dfrac{1}{5} =$

229. $\dfrac{2}{4} + \dfrac{1}{3} =$

230. $\dfrac{5}{6} + \dfrac{3}{4} =$

231. $\dfrac{2}{4} + \dfrac{2}{3} =$

232. $\dfrac{1}{8} + \dfrac{3}{8} =$

233. $\dfrac{1}{6} + \dfrac{2}{3} =$

234. $\dfrac{3}{8} + \dfrac{3}{4} =$

235. $\dfrac{2}{4} + \dfrac{7}{8} =$

236. $\dfrac{7}{8} + \dfrac{3}{5} =$

237. $\dfrac{3}{10} + \dfrac{7}{8} =$

238. $\dfrac{2}{4} + \dfrac{1}{6} =$

239. $\dfrac{9}{10} + \dfrac{4}{5} =$

240. $\dfrac{1}{2} + \dfrac{4}{6} =$

241. $\dfrac{3}{10} + \dfrac{2}{4} =$

242. $\dfrac{3}{6} + \dfrac{3}{4} =$

243. $\dfrac{1}{2} + \dfrac{5}{6} =$

244. $\dfrac{6}{10} + \dfrac{1}{4} =$

245. $\dfrac{1}{2} + \dfrac{3}{5} =$

246. $\dfrac{5}{6} + \dfrac{7}{8} =$

247. $\dfrac{2}{4} + \dfrac{2}{4} =$

248. $\dfrac{1}{8} + \dfrac{2}{3} =$

249. $\dfrac{2}{10} + \dfrac{5}{6} =$

250. $\dfrac{1}{2} + \dfrac{2}{3} =$

251. $\dfrac{3}{10} + \dfrac{2}{6} =$

252. $\dfrac{1}{2} + \dfrac{5}{8} =$

253. $\dfrac{1}{6} + \dfrac{1}{3} =$

254. $\dfrac{2}{4} + \dfrac{1}{5} =$

255. $\dfrac{3}{8} + \dfrac{1}{8} =$

256. $\dfrac{8}{10} + \dfrac{1}{3} =$

257. $\dfrac{3}{4} + \dfrac{3}{8} =$ ....

258. $\dfrac{2}{6} + \dfrac{2}{4} =$ ....

259. $\dfrac{1}{2} + \dfrac{1}{3} =$ ....

260. $\dfrac{3}{10} + \dfrac{1}{5} =$ ....

261. $\dfrac{1}{4} + \dfrac{3}{5} =$ ....

262. $\dfrac{6}{10} + \dfrac{4}{8} =$ ....

263. $\dfrac{7}{8} + \dfrac{1}{5} =$ ....

264. $\dfrac{5}{10} + \dfrac{2}{4} =$ ....

265. $\dfrac{5}{10} + \dfrac{7}{8} =$ ....

266. $\dfrac{6}{8} + \dfrac{3}{4} =$ ....

267. $\dfrac{4}{10} + \dfrac{1}{5} =$ ....

268. $\dfrac{5}{8} + \dfrac{4}{5} =$ ....

269. $\dfrac{5}{10} + \dfrac{6}{8} =$ ....

270. $\dfrac{4}{6} + \dfrac{2}{4} =$ ....

271. $\dfrac{5}{6} + \dfrac{1}{4} =$ ....

272. $\dfrac{1}{4} + \dfrac{2}{3} =$ ....

273. $\dfrac{1}{2} + \dfrac{3}{6} =$

274. $\dfrac{4}{6} + \dfrac{5}{8} =$

275. $\dfrac{8}{10} + \dfrac{1}{5} =$

276. $\dfrac{8}{10} + \dfrac{2}{8} =$

277. $\dfrac{5}{8} + \dfrac{7}{8} =$

278. $\dfrac{7}{10} + \dfrac{4}{6} =$

279. $\dfrac{3}{4} + \dfrac{2}{8} =$

280. $\dfrac{1}{4} + \dfrac{1}{3} =$

281. $\dfrac{1}{2} + \dfrac{1}{5} =$

282. $\dfrac{7}{8} + \dfrac{2}{4} =$

283. $\dfrac{2}{6} + \dfrac{1}{3} =$

284. $\dfrac{5}{8} + \dfrac{1}{4} =$

285. $\dfrac{1}{8} + \dfrac{2}{5} =$

286. $\dfrac{1}{2} + \dfrac{2}{6} =$

287. $\dfrac{6}{8} + \dfrac{2}{3} =$

288. $\dfrac{4}{8} + \dfrac{4}{8} =$

EXERCISES 2

FRACTIONS SUBTRACTION

289. $\dfrac{3}{4} - \dfrac{2}{4} =$ ....

290. $\dfrac{5}{6} - \dfrac{4}{6} =$ ....

291. $\dfrac{4}{5} - \dfrac{3}{5} =$ ....

292. $\dfrac{2}{3} - \dfrac{1}{3} =$ ....

293. $\dfrac{4}{5} - \dfrac{1}{5} =$ ....

294. $\dfrac{2}{4} - \dfrac{1}{4} =$ ....

295. $\dfrac{4}{6} - \dfrac{3}{6} =$ ....

296. $\dfrac{3}{5} - \dfrac{1}{5} =$ ....

297. $\dfrac{5}{6} - \dfrac{2}{6} =$ ....

298. $\dfrac{4}{5} - \dfrac{2}{5} =$ ....

299. $\dfrac{3}{6} - \dfrac{1}{6} =$ ....

300. $\dfrac{3}{4} - \dfrac{1}{4} =$ ....

301. $\dfrac{3}{5} - \dfrac{2}{5} =$ ....

302. $\dfrac{5}{6} - \dfrac{3}{6} =$ ....

303. $\dfrac{4}{6} - \dfrac{1}{6} =$ ....

304. $\dfrac{2}{5} - \dfrac{1}{5} =$ ....

305. $\dfrac{5}{6} - \dfrac{1}{6} =$ ....

306. $\dfrac{3}{6} - \dfrac{2}{6} =$ ....

307. $\dfrac{4}{6} - \dfrac{2}{6} =$ ....

308. $\dfrac{2}{6} - \dfrac{1}{6} =$ ....

309. $\dfrac{2}{3} - \dfrac{1}{3} =$ ....

310. $\dfrac{3}{4} - \dfrac{2}{4} =$ ....

311. $\dfrac{2}{5} - \dfrac{1}{5} =$ ....

312. $\dfrac{4}{5} - \dfrac{3}{5} =$ ....

313. $\dfrac{2}{3} - \dfrac{1}{3} =$ ....

314. $\dfrac{3}{4} - \dfrac{2}{4} =$ ....

315. $\dfrac{3}{4} - \dfrac{1}{4} =$ ....

316. $\dfrac{4}{5} - \dfrac{3}{5} =$ ....

317. $\dfrac{4}{5} - \dfrac{3}{5} =$ ....

318. $\dfrac{2}{5} - \dfrac{1}{5} =$ ....

319. $\dfrac{3}{4} - \dfrac{2}{4} =$ ....

320. $\dfrac{2}{3} - \dfrac{1}{3} =$ ....

321. $\dfrac{2}{3} - \dfrac{1}{3} =$ ....

322. $\dfrac{4}{5} - \dfrac{2}{5} =$ ....

323. $\dfrac{3}{4} - \dfrac{2}{4} =$ ....

324. $\dfrac{3}{4} - \dfrac{1}{4} =$ ....

325. $\dfrac{3}{4} - \dfrac{1}{4} =$ ....

326. $\dfrac{3}{6} - \dfrac{1}{6} =$ ....

327. $\dfrac{5}{6} - \dfrac{4}{6} =$ ....

328. $\dfrac{2}{3} - \dfrac{1}{3} =$ ....

329. $\dfrac{3}{4} - \dfrac{2}{4} =$ ....

330. $\dfrac{2}{3} - \dfrac{1}{3} =$ ....

331. $\dfrac{4}{5} - \dfrac{3}{5} =$ ....

332. $\dfrac{2}{3} - \dfrac{1}{3} =$ ....

333. $\dfrac{4}{5} - \dfrac{3}{5} =$ ....

334. $\dfrac{4}{5} - \dfrac{3}{5} =$ ....

335. $\dfrac{3}{4} - \dfrac{2}{4} =$ ....

336. $\dfrac{2}{4} - \dfrac{1}{4} =$ ....

337. $\dfrac{5}{6} - \dfrac{4}{6} =$

338. $\dfrac{3}{4} - \dfrac{1}{4} =$

339. $\dfrac{4}{6} - \dfrac{3}{6} =$

340. $\dfrac{3}{6} - \dfrac{2}{6} =$

341. $\dfrac{4}{6} - \dfrac{1}{6} =$

342. $\dfrac{4}{5} - \dfrac{2}{5} =$

343. $\dfrac{2}{4} - \dfrac{1}{4} =$

344. $\dfrac{3}{5} - \dfrac{1}{5} =$

345. $\dfrac{3}{4} - \dfrac{2}{4} =$

346. $\dfrac{3}{4} - \dfrac{2}{4} =$

347. $\dfrac{5}{6} - \dfrac{3}{6} =$

348. $\dfrac{3}{4} - \dfrac{2}{4} =$

349. $\dfrac{2}{3} - \dfrac{1}{3} =$

350. $\dfrac{3}{5} - \dfrac{2}{5} =$

351. $\dfrac{3}{4} - \dfrac{2}{4} =$

352. $\dfrac{2}{3} - \dfrac{1}{3} =$

353. $\dfrac{2}{3} - \dfrac{1}{3} =$ ....

354. $\dfrac{2}{5} - \dfrac{1}{5} =$ ....

355. $\dfrac{3}{4} - \dfrac{1}{4} =$ ....

356. $\dfrac{3}{6} - \dfrac{1}{6} =$ ....

357. $\dfrac{4}{5} - \dfrac{1}{5} =$ ....

358. $\dfrac{4}{5} - \dfrac{3}{5} =$ ....

359. $\dfrac{3}{5} - \dfrac{2}{5} =$ ....

360. $\dfrac{2}{3} - \dfrac{1}{3} =$ ....

361. $\dfrac{3}{4} - \dfrac{2}{4} =$ ....

362. $\dfrac{4}{6} - \dfrac{1}{6} =$ ....

363. $\dfrac{4}{6} - \dfrac{3}{6} =$ ....

364. $\dfrac{3}{4} - \dfrac{1}{4} =$ ....

365. $\dfrac{4}{5} - \dfrac{2}{5} =$ ....

366. $\dfrac{2}{3} - \dfrac{1}{3} =$ ....

367. $\dfrac{2}{5} - \dfrac{1}{5} =$ ....

368. $\dfrac{4}{6} - \dfrac{3}{6} =$ ....

369. $\dfrac{3}{6} - \dfrac{2}{6} =$ ....

370. $\dfrac{2}{3} - \dfrac{1}{3} =$ ....

371. $\dfrac{5}{6} - \dfrac{4}{6} =$ ....

372. $\dfrac{3}{6} - \dfrac{2}{6} =$ ....

373. $\dfrac{5}{6} - \dfrac{4}{6} =$ ....

374. $\dfrac{5}{6} - \dfrac{3}{6} =$ ....

375. $\dfrac{2}{3} - \dfrac{1}{3} =$ ....

376. $\dfrac{2}{4} - \dfrac{1}{4} =$ ....

377. $\dfrac{5}{6} - \dfrac{4}{6} =$ ....

378. $\dfrac{4}{6} - \dfrac{2}{6} =$ ....

379. $\dfrac{2}{3} - \dfrac{1}{3} =$ ....

380. $\dfrac{3}{6} - \dfrac{2}{6} =$ ....

381. $\dfrac{2}{3} - \dfrac{1}{3} =$ ....

382. $\dfrac{2}{6} - \dfrac{1}{6} =$ ....

383. $\dfrac{2}{3} - \dfrac{1}{3} =$ ....

384. $\dfrac{2}{3} - \dfrac{1}{3} =$ ....

385. $\dfrac{7}{10} - \dfrac{5}{10} =$ ....

386. $\dfrac{8}{9} - \dfrac{3}{9} =$ ....

387. $\dfrac{6}{7} - \dfrac{4}{7} =$ ....

388. $\dfrac{3}{10} - \dfrac{2}{10} =$ ....

389. $\dfrac{11}{12} - \dfrac{10}{12} =$ ....

390. $\dfrac{4}{8} - \dfrac{2}{8} =$ ....

391. $\dfrac{10}{11} - \dfrac{9}{11} =$ ....

392. $\dfrac{3}{8} - \dfrac{2}{8} =$ ....

393. $\dfrac{8}{10} - \dfrac{4}{10} =$ ....

394. $\dfrac{4}{7} - \dfrac{3}{7} =$ ....

395. $\dfrac{6}{9} - \dfrac{3}{9} =$ ....

396. $\dfrac{7}{11} - \dfrac{3}{11} =$ ....

397. $\dfrac{6}{12} - \dfrac{3}{12} =$ ....

398. $\dfrac{6}{10} - \dfrac{5}{10} =$ ....

399. $\dfrac{3}{12} - \dfrac{2}{12} =$ ....

400. $\dfrac{7}{8} - \dfrac{4}{8} =$ ....

401. $\dfrac{6}{7} - \dfrac{5}{7} =$ ....

402. $\dfrac{6}{11} - \dfrac{4}{11} =$ ....

403. $\dfrac{9}{10} - \dfrac{2}{10} =$ ....

404. $\dfrac{10}{11} - \dfrac{7}{11} =$ ....

405. $\dfrac{6}{7} - \dfrac{3}{7} =$ ....

406. $\dfrac{10}{12} - \dfrac{8}{12} =$ ....

407. $\dfrac{4}{8} - \dfrac{3}{8} =$ ....

408. $\dfrac{2}{9} - \dfrac{1}{9} =$ ....

409. $\dfrac{7}{8} - \dfrac{6}{8} =$ ....

410. $\dfrac{10}{11} - \dfrac{2}{11} =$ ....

411. $\dfrac{8}{9} - \dfrac{2}{9} =$ ....

412. $\dfrac{8}{10} - \dfrac{6}{10} =$ ....

413. $\dfrac{4}{12} - \dfrac{3}{12} =$ ....

414. $\dfrac{7}{10} - \dfrac{4}{10} =$ ....

415. $\dfrac{5}{7} - \dfrac{4}{7} =$ ....

416. $\dfrac{6}{9} - \dfrac{5}{9} =$ ....

417. $\dfrac{9}{12} - \dfrac{6}{12} =$ ....

418. $\dfrac{7}{9} - \dfrac{2}{9} =$ ....

419. $\dfrac{7}{12} - \dfrac{2}{12} =$ ....

420. $\dfrac{9}{10} - \dfrac{6}{10} =$ ....

421. $\dfrac{7}{8} - \dfrac{5}{8} =$ ....

422. $\dfrac{2}{7} - \dfrac{1}{7} =$ ....

423. $\dfrac{8}{11} - \dfrac{2}{11} =$ ....

424. $\dfrac{11}{12} - \dfrac{4}{12} =$ ....

425. $\dfrac{7}{9} - \dfrac{6}{9} =$ ....

426. $\dfrac{6}{12} - \dfrac{5}{12} =$ ....

427. $\dfrac{8}{11} - \dfrac{4}{11} =$ ....

428. $\dfrac{5}{7} - \dfrac{2}{7} =$ ....

429. $\dfrac{4}{9} - \dfrac{2}{9} =$ ....

430. $\dfrac{8}{10} - \dfrac{2}{10} =$ ....

431. $\dfrac{9}{11} - \dfrac{1}{11} =$ ....

432. $\dfrac{11}{12} - \dfrac{8}{12} =$ ....

433. $\dfrac{6}{9} - \dfrac{4}{9} =$

434. $\dfrac{8}{11} - \dfrac{1}{11} =$

435. $\dfrac{7}{8} - \dfrac{3}{8} =$

436. $\dfrac{9}{10} - \dfrac{8}{10} =$

437. $\dfrac{8}{9} - \dfrac{7}{9} =$

438. $\dfrac{6}{12} - \dfrac{2}{12} =$

439. $\dfrac{5}{9} - \dfrac{2}{9} =$

440. $\dfrac{9}{11} - \dfrac{7}{11} =$

441. $\dfrac{11}{12} - \dfrac{9}{12} =$

442. $\dfrac{11}{12} - \dfrac{1}{12} =$

443. $\dfrac{8}{11} - \dfrac{7}{11} =$

444. $\dfrac{6}{10} - \dfrac{3}{10} =$

445. $\dfrac{5}{9} - \dfrac{4}{9} =$

446. $\dfrac{11}{12} - \dfrac{5}{12} =$

447. $\dfrac{9}{11} - \dfrac{5}{11} =$

448. $\dfrac{4}{10} - \dfrac{1}{10} =$

449. $\dfrac{7}{8} - \dfrac{2}{8} =$ ....

450. $\dfrac{6}{8} - \dfrac{4}{8} =$ ....

451. $\dfrac{9}{10} - \dfrac{7}{10} =$ ....

452. $\dfrac{3}{9} - \dfrac{2}{9} =$ ....

453. $\dfrac{9}{11} - \dfrac{4}{11} =$ ....

454. $\dfrac{10}{12} - \dfrac{7}{12} =$ ....

455. $\dfrac{4}{9} - \dfrac{1}{9} =$ ....

456. $\dfrac{9}{11} - \dfrac{6}{11} =$ ....

457. $\dfrac{10}{11} - \dfrac{3}{11} =$ ....

458. $\dfrac{2}{12} - \dfrac{1}{12} =$ ....

459. $\dfrac{6}{7} - \dfrac{1}{7} =$ ....

460. $\dfrac{7}{10} - \dfrac{3}{10} =$ ....

461. $\dfrac{8}{11} - \dfrac{3}{11} =$ ....

462. $\dfrac{9}{10} - \dfrac{4}{10} =$ ....

463. $\dfrac{6}{9} - \dfrac{2}{9} =$ ....

464. $\dfrac{6}{8} - \dfrac{1}{8} =$ ....

465. $\dfrac{10}{12} - \dfrac{6}{12} =$ ....

466. $\dfrac{9}{10} - \dfrac{5}{10} =$ ....

467. $\dfrac{7}{9} - \dfrac{4}{9} =$ ....

468. $\dfrac{5}{8} - \dfrac{4}{8} =$ ....

469. $\dfrac{8}{12} - \dfrac{2}{12} =$ ....

470. $\dfrac{4}{10} - \dfrac{2}{10} =$ ....

471. $\dfrac{4}{12} - \dfrac{1}{12} =$ ....

472. $\dfrac{6}{8} - \dfrac{2}{8} =$ ....

473. $\dfrac{7}{9} - \dfrac{1}{9} =$ ....

474. $\dfrac{5}{10} - \dfrac{4}{10} =$ ....

475. $\dfrac{11}{12} - \dfrac{7}{12} =$ ....

476. $\dfrac{11}{12} - \dfrac{6}{12} =$ ....

477. $\dfrac{6}{7} - \dfrac{2}{7} =$ ....

478. $\dfrac{7}{11} - \dfrac{4}{11} =$ ....

479. $\dfrac{7}{11} - \dfrac{2}{11} =$ ....

480. $\dfrac{7}{10} - \dfrac{6}{10} =$ ....

481. $\dfrac{8}{11} - \dfrac{1}{3} =$ ....

482. $\dfrac{5}{8} - \dfrac{1}{4} =$ ....

483. $\dfrac{8}{9} - \dfrac{7}{8} =$ ....

484. $\dfrac{10}{11} - \dfrac{2}{3} =$ ....

485. $\dfrac{7}{8} - \dfrac{2}{5} =$ ....

486. $\dfrac{9}{12} - \dfrac{2}{8} =$ ....

487. $\dfrac{8}{9} - \dfrac{2}{3} =$ ....

488. $\dfrac{7}{10} - \dfrac{2}{4} =$ ....

489. $\dfrac{9}{11} - \dfrac{1}{6} =$ ....

490. $\dfrac{7}{9} - \dfrac{1}{3} =$ ....

491. $\dfrac{7}{9} - \dfrac{3}{6} =$ ....

492. $\dfrac{2}{7} - \dfrac{1}{5} =$ ....

493. $\dfrac{9}{10} - \dfrac{6}{8} =$ ....

494. $\dfrac{6}{9} - \dfrac{3}{5} =$ ....

495. $\dfrac{9}{10} - \dfrac{2}{3} =$ ....

496. $\dfrac{11}{12} - \dfrac{6}{8} =$ ....

497. $\dfrac{4}{8} - \dfrac{2}{5} =$ ....

498. $\dfrac{5}{9} - \dfrac{1}{8} =$ ....

499. $\dfrac{5}{11} - \dfrac{1}{4} =$ ....

500. $\dfrac{8}{9} - \dfrac{4}{6} =$ ....

501. $\dfrac{6}{7} - \dfrac{4}{5} =$ ....

502. $\dfrac{6}{11} - \dfrac{1}{3} =$ ....

503. $\dfrac{9}{12} - \dfrac{2}{3} =$ ....

504. $\dfrac{4}{10} - \dfrac{1}{4} =$ ....

505. $\dfrac{3}{7} - \dfrac{1}{6} =$ ....

506. $\dfrac{10}{11} - \dfrac{3}{4} =$ ....

507. $\dfrac{6}{7} - \dfrac{4}{8} =$ ....

508. $\dfrac{7}{9} - \dfrac{2}{5} =$ ....

509. $\dfrac{6}{7} - \dfrac{3}{8} =$ ....

510. $\dfrac{2}{8} - \dfrac{1}{5} =$ ....

511. $\dfrac{4}{7} - \dfrac{1}{6} =$ ....

512. $\dfrac{4}{9} - \dfrac{1}{5} =$ ....

513. $\dfrac{4}{7} - \dfrac{1}{5} =$ ....

514. $\dfrac{7}{8} - \dfrac{2}{6} =$ ....

515. $\dfrac{10}{12} - \dfrac{1}{5} =$ ....

516. $\dfrac{7}{11} - \dfrac{1}{3} =$ ....

517. $\dfrac{6}{10} - \dfrac{4}{8} =$ ....

518. $\dfrac{7}{9} - \dfrac{1}{4} =$ ....

519. $\dfrac{5}{9} - \dfrac{1}{6} =$ ....

520. $\dfrac{6}{8} - \dfrac{2}{5} =$ ....

521. $\dfrac{4}{7} - \dfrac{4}{8} =$ ....

522. $\dfrac{5}{8} - \dfrac{3}{5} =$ ....

523. $\dfrac{8}{12} - \dfrac{3}{5} =$ ....

524. $\dfrac{4}{12} - \dfrac{1}{8} =$ ....

525. $\dfrac{9}{11} - \dfrac{2}{5} =$ ....

526. $\dfrac{6}{10} - \dfrac{1}{6} =$ ....

527. $\dfrac{9}{11} - \dfrac{3}{4} =$ ....

528. $\dfrac{6}{9} - \dfrac{1}{6} =$ ....

529. $\dfrac{5}{7} - \dfrac{2}{3} =$ ....

530. $\dfrac{6}{12} - \dfrac{1}{3} =$ ....

531. $\dfrac{9}{12} - \dfrac{1}{5} =$ ....

532. $\dfrac{3}{10} - \dfrac{1}{6} =$ ....

533. $\dfrac{10}{11} - \dfrac{4}{8} =$ ....

534. $\dfrac{2}{8} - \dfrac{1}{6} =$ ....

535. $\dfrac{5}{7} - \dfrac{1}{3} =$ ....

536. $\dfrac{6}{7} - \dfrac{3}{5} =$ ....

537. $\dfrac{7}{11} - \dfrac{1}{6} =$ ....

538. $\dfrac{5}{7} - \dfrac{4}{8} =$ ....

539. $\dfrac{5}{11} - \dfrac{1}{3} =$ ....

540. $\dfrac{7}{10} - \dfrac{3}{5} =$ ....

541. $\dfrac{8}{12} - \dfrac{1}{8} =$ ....

542. $\dfrac{5}{10} - \dfrac{1}{4} =$ ....

543. $\dfrac{6}{7} - \dfrac{1}{3} =$ ....

544. $\dfrac{4}{7} - \dfrac{1}{3} =$ ....

545. $\dfrac{6}{10} - \dfrac{1}{4} =$ ....

546. $\dfrac{9}{11} - \dfrac{2}{8} =$ ....

547. $\dfrac{4}{7} - \dfrac{2}{5} =$ ....

548. $\dfrac{7}{8} - \dfrac{1}{3} =$ ....

549. $\dfrac{3}{10} - \dfrac{1}{5} =$ ....

550. $\dfrac{5}{8} - \dfrac{4}{8} =$ ....

551. $\dfrac{9}{12} - \dfrac{1}{3} =$ ....

552. $\dfrac{4}{11} - \dfrac{2}{6} =$ ....

553. $\dfrac{7}{9} - \dfrac{1}{8} =$ ....

554. $\dfrac{3}{11} - \dfrac{1}{5} =$ ....

555. $\dfrac{8}{9} - \dfrac{3}{8} =$ ....

556. $\dfrac{7}{9} - \dfrac{6}{8} =$ ....

557. $\dfrac{6}{9} - \dfrac{2}{6} =$ ....

558. $\dfrac{9}{10} - \dfrac{3}{4} =$ ....

559. $\dfrac{7}{11} - \dfrac{3}{8} =$ ....

560. $\dfrac{10}{11} - \dfrac{2}{4} =$ ....

561. $\dfrac{8}{10} - \dfrac{3}{5} =$ ....

562. $\dfrac{8}{9} - \dfrac{2}{4} =$ ....

563. $\dfrac{7}{8} - \dfrac{1}{4} =$ ....

564. $\dfrac{9}{12} - \dfrac{1}{6} =$ ....

565. $\dfrac{7}{9} - \dfrac{2}{3} =$ ....

566. $\dfrac{7}{12} - \dfrac{2}{4} =$ ....

567. $\dfrac{6}{9} - \dfrac{2}{5} =$ ....

568. $\dfrac{6}{9} - \dfrac{1}{3} =$ ....

569. $\dfrac{8}{9} - \dfrac{2}{6} =$ ....

570. $\dfrac{9}{10} - \dfrac{2}{4} =$ ....

571. $\dfrac{5}{7} - \dfrac{2}{6} =$ ....

572. $\dfrac{4}{9} - \dfrac{1}{4} =$ ....

573. $\dfrac{7}{9} - \dfrac{1}{5} =$ ....

574. $\dfrac{2}{9} - \dfrac{1}{5} =$ ....

575. $\dfrac{6}{7} - \dfrac{2}{3} =$ ....

576. $\dfrac{4}{8} - \dfrac{2}{6} =$ ....

EXERCISES 3

FRACTIONS MULTIPLICATION

577. $\dfrac{2}{3} \times \dfrac{2}{3} =$ ....

578. $\dfrac{1}{5} \times \dfrac{4}{5} =$ ....

579. $\dfrac{1}{4} \times \dfrac{3}{4} =$ ....

580. $\dfrac{4}{6} \times \dfrac{2}{6} =$ ....

581. $\dfrac{1}{2} \times \dfrac{1}{2} =$ ....

582. $\dfrac{2}{5} \times \dfrac{1}{5} =$ ....

583. $\dfrac{3}{4} \times \dfrac{3}{4} =$ ....

584. $\dfrac{5}{6} \times \dfrac{5}{6} =$ ....

585. $\dfrac{2}{3} \times \dfrac{1}{3} =$ ....

586. $\dfrac{1}{6} \times \dfrac{2}{6} =$ ....

587. $\dfrac{1}{5} \times \dfrac{2}{5} =$ ....

588. $\dfrac{1}{4} \times \dfrac{1}{4} =$ ....

589. $\dfrac{4}{6} \times \dfrac{5}{6} =$ ....

590. $\dfrac{3}{5} \times \dfrac{4}{5} =$ ....

591. $\dfrac{1}{3} \times \dfrac{1}{3} =$ ....

592. $\dfrac{4}{6} \times \dfrac{1}{6} =$ ....

593. $\dfrac{1}{5} \times \dfrac{3}{5} =$ ....

594. $\dfrac{1}{3} \times \dfrac{2}{3} =$ ....

595. $\dfrac{3}{5} \times \dfrac{2}{5} =$ ....

596. $\dfrac{4}{6} \times \dfrac{3}{6} =$ ....

597. $\dfrac{1}{6} \times \dfrac{3}{6} =$ ....

598. $\dfrac{3}{4} \times \dfrac{1}{4} =$ ....

599. $\dfrac{1}{5} \times \dfrac{1}{5} =$ ....

600. $\dfrac{2}{4} \times \dfrac{3}{4} =$ ....

601. $\dfrac{4}{5} \times \dfrac{1}{5} =$ ....

602. $\dfrac{2}{4} \times \dfrac{2}{4} =$ ....

603. $\dfrac{5}{6} \times \dfrac{2}{6} =$ ....

604. $\dfrac{2}{5} \times \dfrac{2}{5} =$ ....

605. $\dfrac{3}{6} \times \dfrac{5}{6} =$ ....

606. $\dfrac{2}{5} \times \dfrac{4}{5} =$ ....

607. $\dfrac{3}{6} \times \dfrac{3}{6} =$ ....

608. $\dfrac{4}{5} \times \dfrac{3}{5} =$ ....

609. $\dfrac{2}{6} \times \dfrac{4}{6} =$ ....

610. $\dfrac{3}{6} \times \dfrac{2}{6} =$ ....

611. $\dfrac{1}{6} \times \dfrac{1}{6} =$ ....

612. $\dfrac{3}{4} \times \dfrac{2}{4} =$ ....

613. $\dfrac{3}{6} \times \dfrac{1}{6} =$ ....

614. $\dfrac{1}{6} \times \dfrac{4}{6} =$ ....

615. $\dfrac{2}{5} \times \dfrac{3}{5} =$ ....

616. $\dfrac{1}{4} \times \dfrac{2}{4} =$ ....

617. $\dfrac{3}{5} \times \dfrac{1}{5} =$ ....

618. $\dfrac{4}{5} \times \dfrac{2}{5} =$ ....

619. $\dfrac{2}{6} \times \dfrac{2}{6} =$ ....

620. $\dfrac{2}{6} \times \dfrac{3}{6} =$ ....

621. $\dfrac{4}{5} \times \dfrac{4}{5} =$ ....

622. $\dfrac{2}{6} \times \dfrac{1}{6} =$ ....

623. $\dfrac{1}{6} \times \dfrac{5}{6} =$ ....

624. $\dfrac{2}{6} \times \dfrac{5}{6} =$ ....

625. $\dfrac{2}{4} \times \dfrac{1}{4} =$ ....

626. $\dfrac{5}{6} \times \dfrac{4}{6} =$ ....

627. $\dfrac{3}{6} \times \dfrac{4}{6} =$ ....

628. $\dfrac{4}{6} \times \dfrac{4}{6} =$ ....

629. $\dfrac{5}{6} \times \dfrac{1}{6} =$ ....

630. $\dfrac{3}{5} \times \dfrac{3}{5} =$ ....

631. $\dfrac{5}{6} \times \dfrac{3}{6} =$ ....

632. $\dfrac{1}{2} \times \dfrac{1}{2} =$ ....

633. $\dfrac{4}{6} \times \dfrac{4}{6} =$ ....

634. $\dfrac{2}{4} \times \dfrac{3}{4} =$ ....

635. $\dfrac{3}{5} \times \dfrac{2}{5} =$ ....

636. $\dfrac{1}{5} \times \dfrac{2}{5} =$ ....

637. $\dfrac{2}{3} \times \dfrac{2}{3} =$ ....

638. $\dfrac{2}{4} \times \dfrac{1}{4} =$ ....

639. $\dfrac{1}{2} \times \dfrac{1}{2} =$ ....

640. $\dfrac{1}{4} \times \dfrac{2}{4} =$ ....

641. $\dfrac{2}{6} \times \dfrac{1}{6} =$ ....

642. $\dfrac{2}{3} \times \dfrac{1}{3} =$ ....

643. $\dfrac{4}{6} \times \dfrac{2}{6} =$ ....

644. $\dfrac{1}{2} \times \dfrac{1}{2} =$ ....

645. $\dfrac{2}{4} \times \dfrac{1}{4} =$ ....

646. $\dfrac{1}{2} \times \dfrac{1}{2} =$ ....

647. $\dfrac{1}{2} \times \dfrac{1}{2} =$ ....

648. $\dfrac{2}{5} \times \dfrac{3}{5} =$ ....

649. $\dfrac{1}{2} \times \dfrac{1}{2} =$ ....

650. $\dfrac{1}{2} \times \dfrac{1}{2} =$ ....

651. $\dfrac{4}{6} \times \dfrac{4}{6} =$ ....

652. $\dfrac{2}{5} \times \dfrac{3}{5} =$ ....

653. $\dfrac{1}{2} \times \dfrac{1}{2} =$ ....

654. $\dfrac{1}{4} \times \dfrac{2}{4} =$ ....

655. $\dfrac{2}{6} \times \dfrac{1}{6} =$ ....

656. $\dfrac{5}{6} \times \dfrac{1}{6} =$ ....

657. $\dfrac{1}{2} \times \dfrac{1}{2} =$ ....

658. $\dfrac{2}{4} \times \dfrac{3}{4} =$ ....

659. $\dfrac{1}{3} \times \dfrac{2}{3} =$ ....

660. $\dfrac{2}{6} \times \dfrac{1}{6} =$ ....

661. $\dfrac{2}{6} \times \dfrac{4}{6} =$ ....

662. $\dfrac{1}{3} \times \dfrac{2}{3} =$ ....

663. $\dfrac{1}{2} \times \dfrac{1}{2} =$ ....

664. $\dfrac{4}{5} \times \dfrac{3}{5} =$ ....

665. $\dfrac{2}{5} \times \dfrac{4}{5} =$ ....

666. $\dfrac{1}{5} \times \dfrac{3}{5} =$ ....

667. $\dfrac{1}{2} \times \dfrac{1}{2} =$ ....

668. $\dfrac{2}{6} \times \dfrac{1}{6} =$ ....

669. $\dfrac{1}{2} \times \dfrac{1}{2} =$ ....

670. $\dfrac{1}{2} \times \dfrac{1}{2} =$ ....

671. $\dfrac{2}{5} \times \dfrac{4}{5} =$ ....

672. $\dfrac{2}{6} \times \dfrac{2}{6} =$ ....

673. $\dfrac{5}{9} \times \dfrac{1}{9} =$ ....

674. $\dfrac{5}{7} \times \dfrac{6}{7} =$ ....

675. $\dfrac{7}{10} \times \dfrac{6}{10} =$ ....

676. $\dfrac{4}{11} \times \dfrac{5}{11} =$ ....

677. $\dfrac{7}{9} \times \dfrac{3}{9} =$ ....

678. $\dfrac{2}{11} \times \dfrac{10}{11} =$ ....

679. $\dfrac{2}{7} \times \dfrac{2}{7} =$ ....

680. $\dfrac{3}{8} \times \dfrac{3}{8} =$ ....

681. $\dfrac{5}{10} \times \dfrac{7}{10} =$ ....

682. $\dfrac{4}{9} \times \dfrac{4}{9} =$ ....

683. $\dfrac{7}{8} \times \dfrac{5}{8} =$ ....

684. $\dfrac{2}{7} \times \dfrac{3}{7} =$ ....

685. $\dfrac{3}{11} \times \dfrac{7}{11} =$ ....

686. $\dfrac{9}{11} \times \dfrac{2}{11} =$ ....

687. $\dfrac{1}{8} \times \dfrac{1}{8} =$ ....

688. $\dfrac{1}{9} \times \dfrac{3}{9} =$ ....

689. $\dfrac{2}{10} \times \dfrac{8}{10} =$

690. $\dfrac{1}{7} \times \dfrac{3}{7} =$

691. $\dfrac{7}{9} \times \dfrac{7}{9} =$

692. $\dfrac{1}{11} \times \dfrac{5}{11} =$

693. $\dfrac{4}{7} \times \dfrac{3}{7} =$

694. $\dfrac{9}{10} \times \dfrac{9}{10} =$

695. $\dfrac{3}{8} \times \dfrac{4}{8} =$

696. $\dfrac{5}{10} \times \dfrac{5}{10} =$

697. $\dfrac{1}{8} \times \dfrac{6}{8} =$

698. $\dfrac{4}{7} \times \dfrac{1}{7} =$

699. $\dfrac{2}{11} \times \dfrac{8}{11} =$

700. $\dfrac{2}{9} \times \dfrac{8}{9} =$

701. $\dfrac{6}{8} \times \dfrac{2}{8} =$

702. $\dfrac{6}{9} \times \dfrac{1}{9} =$

703. $\dfrac{5}{7} \times \dfrac{2}{7} =$

704. $\dfrac{4}{10} \times \dfrac{7}{10} =$

705. $\dfrac{3}{11} \times \dfrac{9}{11} =$ ....

706. $\dfrac{7}{10} \times \dfrac{5}{10} =$ ....

707. $\dfrac{2}{11} \times \dfrac{9}{11} =$ ....

708. $\dfrac{3}{7} \times \dfrac{4}{7} =$ ....

709. $\dfrac{5}{8} \times \dfrac{1}{8} =$ ....

710. $\dfrac{8}{9} \times \dfrac{5}{9} =$ ....

711. $\dfrac{5}{7} \times \dfrac{3}{7} =$ ....

712. $\dfrac{1}{9} \times \dfrac{7}{9} =$ ....

713. $\dfrac{2}{11} \times \dfrac{4}{11} =$ ....

714. $\dfrac{2}{8} \times \dfrac{2}{8} =$ ....

715. $\dfrac{5}{10} \times \dfrac{9}{10} =$ ....

716. $\dfrac{6}{10} \times \dfrac{6}{10} =$ ....

717. $\dfrac{3}{11} \times \dfrac{1}{11} =$ ....

718. $\dfrac{6}{9} \times \dfrac{3}{9} =$ ....

719. $\dfrac{1}{7} \times \dfrac{2}{7} =$ ....

720. $\dfrac{7}{11} \times \dfrac{5}{11} =$ ....

721. $\dfrac{7}{9} \times \dfrac{8}{9} =$ ....

722. $\dfrac{4}{10} \times \dfrac{2}{10} =$ ....

723. $\dfrac{3}{8} \times \dfrac{7}{8} =$ ....

724. $\dfrac{4}{9} \times \dfrac{1}{9} =$ ....

725. $\dfrac{6}{8} \times \dfrac{5}{8} =$ ....

726. $\dfrac{3}{10} \times \dfrac{4}{10} =$ ....

727. $\dfrac{1}{7} \times \dfrac{6}{7} =$ ....

728. $\dfrac{9}{11} \times \dfrac{4}{11} =$ ....

729. $\dfrac{10}{11} \times \dfrac{1}{11} =$ ....

730. $\dfrac{2}{8} \times \dfrac{3}{8} =$ ....

731. $\dfrac{8}{10} \times \dfrac{3}{10} =$ ....

732. $\dfrac{6}{7} \times \dfrac{1}{7} =$ ....

733. $\dfrac{2}{9} \times \dfrac{7}{9} =$ ....

734. $\dfrac{4}{10} \times \dfrac{6}{10} =$ ....

735. $\dfrac{5}{11} \times \dfrac{5}{11} =$ ....

736. $\dfrac{7}{9} \times \dfrac{5}{9} =$ ....

737. $\dfrac{7}{8} \times \dfrac{2}{8} =$ ....

738. $\dfrac{8}{9} \times \dfrac{4}{9} =$ ....

739. $\dfrac{3}{7} \times \dfrac{6}{7} =$ ....

740. $\dfrac{7}{11} \times \dfrac{10}{11} =$ ....

741. $\dfrac{7}{10} \times \dfrac{3}{10} =$ ....

742. $\dfrac{3}{8} \times \dfrac{1}{8} =$ ....

743. $\dfrac{1}{10} \times \dfrac{3}{10} =$ ....

744. $\dfrac{6}{9} \times \dfrac{5}{9} =$ ....

745. $\dfrac{5}{8} \times \dfrac{7}{8} =$ ....

746. $\dfrac{8}{10} \times \dfrac{6}{10} =$ ....

747. $\dfrac{2}{7} \times \dfrac{5}{7} =$ ....

748. $\dfrac{10}{11} \times \dfrac{9}{11} =$ ....

749. $\dfrac{4}{8} \times \dfrac{1}{8} =$ ....

750. $\dfrac{2}{7} \times \dfrac{6}{7} =$ ....

751. $\dfrac{3}{9} \times \dfrac{1}{9} =$ ....

752. $\dfrac{5}{11} \times \dfrac{10}{11} =$ ....

753. $\dfrac{2}{8} \times \dfrac{6}{8} =$ ....

754. $\dfrac{9}{10} \times \dfrac{5}{10} =$ ....

755. $\dfrac{2}{7} \times \dfrac{4}{7} =$ ....

756. $\dfrac{6}{9} \times \dfrac{8}{9} =$ ....

757. $\dfrac{6}{11} \times \dfrac{6}{11} =$ ....

758. $\dfrac{1}{10} \times \dfrac{4}{10} =$ ....

759. $\dfrac{9}{11} \times \dfrac{3}{11} =$ ....

760. $\dfrac{3}{9} \times \dfrac{7}{9} =$ ....

761. $\dfrac{1}{10} \times \dfrac{9}{10} =$ ....

762. $\dfrac{4}{9} \times \dfrac{7}{9} =$ ....

763. $\dfrac{7}{8} \times \dfrac{6}{8} =$ ....

764. $\dfrac{5}{11} \times \dfrac{2}{11} =$ ....

765. $\dfrac{6}{8} \times \dfrac{7}{8} =$ ....

766. $\dfrac{8}{10} \times \dfrac{4}{10} =$ ....

767. $\dfrac{7}{11} \times \dfrac{1}{11} =$ ....

768. $\dfrac{3}{9} \times \dfrac{3}{9} =$ ....

769. $\frac{1}{6} \times \frac{2}{4} =$ ....

770. $\frac{2}{3} \times \frac{1}{2} =$ ....

771. $\frac{4}{5} \times \frac{2}{3} =$ ....

772. $\frac{1}{2} \times \frac{1}{2} =$ ....

773. $\frac{2}{6} \times \frac{1}{4} =$ ....

774. $\frac{1}{3} \times \frac{2}{5} =$ ....

775. $\frac{2}{5} \times \frac{1}{2} =$ ....

776. $\frac{1}{2} \times \frac{3}{6} =$ ....

777. $\frac{2}{4} \times \frac{1}{4} =$ ....

778. $\frac{3}{4} \times \frac{1}{3} =$ ....

779. $\frac{3}{5} \times \frac{3}{4} =$ ....

780. $\frac{1}{4} \times \frac{3}{5} =$ ....

781. $\frac{5}{6} \times \frac{2}{6} =$ ....

782. $\frac{5}{6} \times \frac{4}{5} =$ ....

783. $\frac{2}{4} \times \frac{2}{3} =$ ....

784. $\frac{1}{2} \times \frac{2}{3} =$ ....

785. $\dfrac{1}{2} \times \dfrac{3}{4} =$ ....

786. $\dfrac{3}{6} \times \dfrac{4}{5} =$ ....

787. $\dfrac{2}{3} \times \dfrac{5}{6} =$ ....

788. $\dfrac{3}{4} \times \dfrac{3}{4} =$ ....

789. $\dfrac{1}{3} \times \dfrac{2}{3} =$ ....

790. $\dfrac{3}{4} \times \dfrac{1}{2} =$ ....

791. $\dfrac{5}{6} \times \dfrac{3}{6} =$ ....

792. $\dfrac{1}{2} \times \dfrac{1}{4} =$ ....

793. $\dfrac{1}{4} \times \dfrac{5}{6} =$ ....

794. $\dfrac{1}{3} \times \dfrac{1}{4} =$ ....

795. $\dfrac{1}{6} \times \dfrac{2}{5} =$ ....

796. $\dfrac{1}{2} \times \dfrac{4}{6} =$ ....

797. $\dfrac{3}{5} \times \dfrac{3}{5} =$ ....

798. $\dfrac{5}{6} \times \dfrac{2}{3} =$ ....

799. $\dfrac{1}{2} \times \dfrac{1}{3} =$ ....

800. $\dfrac{3}{5} \times \dfrac{4}{5} =$ ....

801. $\dfrac{2}{3} \times \dfrac{3}{4} =$ ....

802. $\dfrac{2}{5} \times \dfrac{2}{6} =$ ....

803. $\dfrac{2}{4} \times \dfrac{5}{6} =$ ....

804. $\dfrac{1}{6} \times \dfrac{2}{6} =$ ....

805. $\dfrac{4}{6} \times \dfrac{4}{5} =$ ....

806. $\dfrac{2}{5} \times \dfrac{2}{4} =$ ....

807. $\dfrac{1}{3} \times \dfrac{3}{4} =$ ....

808. $\dfrac{4}{6} \times \dfrac{1}{2} =$ ....

809. $\dfrac{3}{5} \times \dfrac{2}{3} =$ ....

810. $\dfrac{1}{2} \times \dfrac{5}{6} =$ ....

811. $\dfrac{1}{4} \times \dfrac{2}{3} =$ ....

812. $\dfrac{2}{3} \times \dfrac{1}{4} =$ ....

813. $\dfrac{2}{5} \times \dfrac{3}{6} =$ ....

814. $\dfrac{2}{3} \times \dfrac{4}{5} =$ ....

815. $\dfrac{1}{3} \times \dfrac{1}{6} =$ ....

816. $\dfrac{5}{6} \times \dfrac{4}{6} =$ ....

817. $\dfrac{1}{3} \times \dfrac{1}{2} =$

818. $\dfrac{4}{5} \times \dfrac{1}{3} =$

819. $\dfrac{1}{5} \times \dfrac{1}{2} =$

820. $\dfrac{5}{6} \times \dfrac{1}{2} =$

821. $\dfrac{2}{3} \times \dfrac{1}{5} =$

822. $\dfrac{1}{5} \times \dfrac{1}{4} =$

823. $\dfrac{4}{6} \times \dfrac{1}{5} =$

824. $\dfrac{1}{5} \times \dfrac{2}{3} =$

825. $\dfrac{2}{6} \times \dfrac{1}{2} =$

826. $\dfrac{1}{6} \times \dfrac{5}{6} =$

827. $\dfrac{1}{5} \times \dfrac{3}{4} =$

828. $\dfrac{3}{5} \times \dfrac{3}{6} =$

829. $\dfrac{4}{5} \times \dfrac{2}{5} =$

830. $\dfrac{3}{6} \times \dfrac{1}{2} =$

831. $\dfrac{1}{2} \times \dfrac{2}{6} =$

832. $\dfrac{2}{3} \times \dfrac{1}{6} =$

833. $\dfrac{1}{2} \times \dfrac{3}{5} =$ ....

834. $\dfrac{3}{4} \times \dfrac{5}{6} =$ ....

835. $\dfrac{2}{3} \times \dfrac{3}{5} =$ ....

836. $\dfrac{4}{6} \times \dfrac{4}{6} =$ ....

837. $\dfrac{5}{6} \times \dfrac{2}{5} =$ ....

838. $\dfrac{2}{3} \times \dfrac{2}{6} =$ ....

839. $\dfrac{1}{2} \times \dfrac{2}{4} =$ ....

840. $\dfrac{3}{5} \times \dfrac{2}{6} =$ ....

841. $\dfrac{3}{5} \times \dfrac{1}{2} =$ ....

842. $\dfrac{2}{5} \times \dfrac{2}{5} =$ ....

843. $\dfrac{3}{4} \times \dfrac{1}{6} =$ ....

844. $\dfrac{5}{6} \times \dfrac{1}{3} =$ ....

845. $\dfrac{2}{6} \times \dfrac{4}{6} =$ ....

846. $\dfrac{1}{2} \times \dfrac{4}{5} =$ ....

847. $\dfrac{1}{5} \times \dfrac{1}{6} =$ ....

848. $\dfrac{1}{3} \times \dfrac{3}{5} =$ ....

849. $\dfrac{3}{6} \times \dfrac{1}{3} =$ ....

850. $\dfrac{1}{5} \times \dfrac{4}{5} =$ ....

851. $\dfrac{4}{5} \times \dfrac{1}{2} =$ ....

852. $\dfrac{3}{4} \times \dfrac{2}{4} =$ ....

853. $\dfrac{1}{4} \times \dfrac{1}{2} =$ ....

854. $\dfrac{1}{3} \times \dfrac{3}{6} =$ ....

855. $\dfrac{1}{4} \times \dfrac{4}{6} =$ ....

856. $\dfrac{2}{3} \times \dfrac{3}{6} =$ ....

857. $\dfrac{3}{4} \times \dfrac{2}{5} =$ ....

858. $\dfrac{4}{5} \times \dfrac{3}{6} =$ ....

859. $\dfrac{1}{4} \times \dfrac{3}{4} =$ ....

860. $\dfrac{2}{3} \times \dfrac{2}{4} =$ ....

861. $\dfrac{2}{5} \times \dfrac{4}{5} =$ ....

862. $\dfrac{1}{6} \times \dfrac{1}{2} =$ ....

863. $\dfrac{2}{6} \times \dfrac{2}{3} =$ ....

864. $\dfrac{2}{4} \times \dfrac{1}{2} =$ ....

EXERCISES 4

FRACTIONS DIVISION

865. $\dfrac{2}{6} \div \dfrac{2}{6} =$ ....

866. $\dfrac{1}{4} \div \dfrac{3}{4} =$ ....

867. $\dfrac{2}{5} \div \dfrac{2}{5} =$ ....

868. $\dfrac{3}{6} \div \dfrac{5}{6} =$ ....

869. $\dfrac{1}{2} \div \dfrac{1}{2} =$ ....

870. $\dfrac{3}{4} \div \dfrac{1}{4} =$ ....

871. $\dfrac{3}{6} \div \dfrac{1}{6} =$ ....

872. $\dfrac{3}{5} \div \dfrac{1}{5} =$ ....

873. $\dfrac{1}{3} \div \dfrac{1}{3} =$ ....

874. $\dfrac{2}{3} \div \dfrac{1}{3} =$ ....

875. $\dfrac{4}{6} \div \dfrac{2}{6} =$ ....

876. $\dfrac{1}{4} \div \dfrac{1}{4} =$ ....

877. $\dfrac{2}{5} \div \dfrac{4}{5} =$ ....

878. $\dfrac{1}{6} \div \dfrac{1}{6} =$ ....

879. $\dfrac{3}{5} \div \dfrac{3}{5} =$ ....

880. $\dfrac{3}{4} \div \dfrac{3}{4} =$ ....

881. $\dfrac{5}{6} \div \dfrac{3}{6} =$ ....

882. $\dfrac{2}{4} \div \dfrac{1}{4} =$ ....

883. $\dfrac{3}{6} \div \dfrac{4}{6} =$ ....

884. $\dfrac{3}{5} \div \dfrac{4}{5} =$ ....

885. $\dfrac{1}{6} \div \dfrac{2}{6} =$ ....

886. $\dfrac{2}{4} \div \dfrac{3}{4} =$ ....

887. $\dfrac{4}{6} \div \dfrac{1}{6} =$ ....

888. $\dfrac{4}{5} \div \dfrac{4}{5} =$ ....

889. $\dfrac{2}{4} \div \dfrac{2}{4} =$ ....

890. $\dfrac{5}{6} \div \dfrac{4}{6} =$ ....

891. $\dfrac{4}{5} \div \dfrac{2}{5} =$ ....

892. $\dfrac{3}{6} \div \dfrac{2}{6} =$ ....

893. $\dfrac{2}{3} \div \dfrac{2}{3} =$ ....

894. $\dfrac{3}{4} \div \dfrac{2}{4} =$ ....

895. $\dfrac{4}{6} \div \dfrac{4}{6} =$ ....

896. $\dfrac{5}{6} \div \dfrac{1}{6} =$ ....

897. $\dfrac{4}{5} \div \dfrac{3}{5} =$ ....

898. $\dfrac{1}{5} \div \dfrac{1}{5} =$ ....

899. $\dfrac{1}{4} \div \dfrac{2}{4} =$ ....

900. $\dfrac{5}{6} \div \dfrac{5}{6} =$ ....

901. $\dfrac{1}{3} \div \dfrac{2}{3} =$ ....

902. $\dfrac{2}{6} \div \dfrac{3}{6} =$ ....

903. $\dfrac{1}{5} \div \dfrac{2}{5} =$ ....

904. $\dfrac{3}{6} \div \dfrac{3}{6} =$ ....

905. $\dfrac{4}{6} \div \dfrac{3}{6} =$ ....

906. $\dfrac{1}{5} \div \dfrac{4}{5} =$ ....

907. $\dfrac{1}{5} \div \dfrac{3}{5} =$ ....

908. $\dfrac{2}{6} \div \dfrac{4}{6} =$ ....

909. $\dfrac{3}{5} \div \dfrac{2}{5} =$ ....

910. $\dfrac{1}{6} \div \dfrac{4}{6} =$ ....

911. $\dfrac{2}{5} \div \dfrac{1}{5} =$ ....

912. $\dfrac{1}{6} \div \dfrac{5}{6} =$ ....

913. $\dfrac{1}{6} \div \dfrac{3}{6} =$ ....

914. $\dfrac{2}{5} \div \dfrac{3}{5} =$ ....

915. $\dfrac{2}{6} \div \dfrac{5}{6} =$ ....

916. $\dfrac{4}{5} \div \dfrac{1}{5} =$ ....

917. $\dfrac{4}{6} \div \dfrac{5}{6} =$ ....

918. $\dfrac{5}{6} \div \dfrac{2}{6} =$ ....

919. $\dfrac{2}{6} \div \dfrac{1}{6} =$ ....

920. $\dfrac{1}{2} \div \dfrac{1}{2} =$ ....

921. $\dfrac{2}{5} \div \dfrac{2}{5} =$ ....

922. $\dfrac{1}{2} \div \dfrac{1}{2} =$ ....

923. $\dfrac{1}{5} \div \dfrac{2}{5} =$ ....

924. $\dfrac{1}{3} \div \dfrac{1}{3} =$ ....

925. $\dfrac{2}{6} \div \dfrac{5}{6} =$ ....

926. $\dfrac{1}{3} \div \dfrac{1}{3} =$ ....

927. $\dfrac{3}{6} \div \dfrac{1}{6} =$ ....

928. $\dfrac{5}{6} \div \dfrac{4}{6} =$ ....

929. $\dfrac{1}{5} \div \dfrac{2}{5} =$ ....

930. $\dfrac{3}{6} \div \dfrac{4}{6} =$ ....

931. $\dfrac{1}{2} \div \dfrac{1}{2} =$ ....

932. $\dfrac{2}{5} \div \dfrac{3}{5} =$ ....

933. $\dfrac{1}{3} \div \dfrac{1}{3} =$ ....

934. $\dfrac{3}{6} \div \dfrac{3}{6} =$ ....

935. $\dfrac{1}{3} \div \dfrac{2}{3} =$ ....

936. $\dfrac{2}{6} \div \dfrac{5}{6} =$ ....

937. $\dfrac{1}{3} \div \dfrac{1}{3} =$ ....

938. $\dfrac{3}{4} \div \dfrac{3}{4} =$ ....

939. $\dfrac{5}{6} \div \dfrac{1}{6} =$ ....

940. $\dfrac{1}{4} \div \dfrac{3}{4} =$ ....

941. $\dfrac{1}{5} \div \dfrac{2}{5} =$ ....

942. $\dfrac{1}{3} \div \dfrac{1}{3} =$ ....

943. $\dfrac{2}{4} \div \dfrac{1}{4} =$ ....

944. $\dfrac{1}{6} \div \dfrac{3}{6} =$ ....

945. $\dfrac{2}{5} \div \dfrac{3}{5} =$ ....

946. $\dfrac{1}{3} \div \dfrac{1}{3} =$ ....

947. $\dfrac{5}{6} \div \dfrac{1}{6} =$ ....

948. $\dfrac{1}{5} \div \dfrac{4}{5} =$ ....

949. $\dfrac{2}{5} \div \dfrac{2}{5} =$ ....

950. $\dfrac{5}{6} \div \dfrac{3}{6} =$ ....

951. $\dfrac{5}{6} \div \dfrac{2}{6} =$ ....

952. $\dfrac{3}{4} \div \dfrac{2}{4} =$ ....

953. $\dfrac{2}{5} \div \dfrac{4}{5} =$ ....

954. $\dfrac{1}{4} \div \dfrac{1}{4} =$ ....

955. $\dfrac{3}{5} \div \dfrac{4}{5} =$ ....

956. $\dfrac{1}{6} \div \dfrac{5}{6} =$ ....

957. $\dfrac{1}{2} \div \dfrac{1}{2} =$ ....

958. $\dfrac{1}{2} \div \dfrac{1}{2} =$ ....

959. $\dfrac{4}{5} \div \dfrac{4}{5} =$ ....

960. $\dfrac{2}{5} \div \dfrac{3}{5} =$ ....

961. $\dfrac{4}{7} \div \dfrac{2}{7} =$ ....

962. $\dfrac{2}{9} \div \dfrac{6}{9} =$ ....

963. $\dfrac{3}{11} \div \dfrac{3}{11} =$ ....

964. $\dfrac{4}{10} \div \dfrac{4}{10} =$ ....

965. $\dfrac{3}{8} \div \dfrac{3}{8} =$ ....

966. $\dfrac{8}{9} \div \dfrac{8}{9} =$ ....

967. $\dfrac{6}{7} \div \dfrac{3}{7} =$ ....

968. $\dfrac{3}{7} \div \dfrac{6}{7} =$ ....

969. $\dfrac{8}{9} \div \dfrac{7}{9} =$ ....

970. $\dfrac{6}{11} \div \dfrac{2}{11} =$ ....

971. $\dfrac{1}{10} \div \dfrac{1}{10} =$ ....

972. $\dfrac{5}{8} \div \dfrac{5}{8} =$ ....

973. $\dfrac{1}{7} \div \dfrac{2}{7} =$ ....

974. $\dfrac{3}{11} \div \dfrac{10}{11} =$ ....

975. $\dfrac{4}{9} \div \dfrac{5}{9} =$ ....

976. $\dfrac{5}{8} \div \dfrac{1}{8} =$ ....

977. $\dfrac{4}{10} \div \dfrac{8}{10} =$ ....

978. $\dfrac{5}{7} \div \dfrac{3}{7} =$ ....

979. $\dfrac{3}{11} \div \dfrac{7}{11} =$ ....

980. $\dfrac{6}{10} \div \dfrac{3}{10} =$ ....

981. $\dfrac{5}{9} \div \dfrac{4}{9} =$ ....

982. $\dfrac{3}{8} \div \dfrac{2}{8} =$ ....

983. $\dfrac{8}{11} \div \dfrac{3}{11} =$ ....

984. $\dfrac{2}{7} \div \dfrac{1}{7} =$ ....

985. $\dfrac{4}{8} \div \dfrac{5}{8} =$ ....

986. $\dfrac{6}{10} \div \dfrac{1}{10} =$ ....

987. $\dfrac{3}{9} \div \dfrac{1}{9} =$ ....

988. $\dfrac{4}{7} \div \dfrac{4}{7} =$ ....

989. $\dfrac{6}{9} \div \dfrac{5}{9} =$ ....

990. $\dfrac{6}{11} \div \dfrac{10}{11} =$ ....

991. $\dfrac{9}{10} \div \dfrac{4}{10} =$ ....

992. $\dfrac{7}{8} \div \dfrac{6}{8} =$ ....

993. $\dfrac{7}{11} \div \dfrac{9}{11} =$ ....

994. $\dfrac{5}{9} \div \dfrac{1}{9} =$ ....

995. $\dfrac{6}{10} \div \dfrac{9}{10} =$ ....

996. $\dfrac{5}{8} \div \dfrac{2}{8} =$ ....

997. $\dfrac{2}{7} \div \dfrac{2}{7} =$ ....

998. $\dfrac{6}{9} \div \dfrac{4}{9} =$ ....

999. $\dfrac{7}{8} \div \dfrac{7}{8} =$ ....

1000. $\dfrac{1}{10} \div \dfrac{3}{10} =$ ....

1001. $\dfrac{5}{11} \div \dfrac{8}{11} =$ ....

1002. $\dfrac{10}{11} \div \dfrac{7}{11} =$ ....

1003. $\dfrac{7}{10} \div \dfrac{3}{10} =$ ....

1004. $\dfrac{2}{8} \div \dfrac{2}{8} =$ ....

1005. $\dfrac{5}{7} \div \dfrac{5}{7} =$ ....

1006. $\dfrac{1}{9} \div \dfrac{5}{9} =$ ....

1007. $\dfrac{3}{10} \div \dfrac{2}{10} =$ ....

1008. $\dfrac{5}{9} \div \dfrac{7}{9} =$ ....

1009. $\dfrac{8}{11} \div \dfrac{2}{11} =$ ....

1010. $\dfrac{3}{8} \div \dfrac{4}{8} =$ ....

1011. $\dfrac{6}{8} \div \dfrac{1}{8} =$ ....

1012. $\dfrac{8}{10} \div \dfrac{3}{10} =$ ....

1013. $\dfrac{6}{11} \div \dfrac{7}{11} =$ ....

1014. $\dfrac{8}{9} \div \dfrac{6}{9} =$ ....

1015. $\dfrac{9}{10} \div \dfrac{1}{10} =$ ....

1016. $\dfrac{6}{7} \div \dfrac{1}{7} =$ ....

1017. $\dfrac{8}{10} \div \dfrac{4}{10} =$ ....

1018. $\dfrac{2}{7} \div \dfrac{4}{7} =$ ....

1019. $\dfrac{7}{8} \div \dfrac{3}{8} =$ ....

1020. $\dfrac{8}{9} \div \dfrac{2}{9} =$ ....

1021. $\dfrac{2}{7} \div \dfrac{5}{7} =$ ....

1022. $\dfrac{8}{10} \div \dfrac{9}{10} =$ ....

1023. $\dfrac{8}{11} \div \dfrac{7}{11} =$ ....

1024. $\dfrac{7}{9} \div \dfrac{6}{9} =$ ....

1025. $\dfrac{3}{7} \div \dfrac{3}{7} =$ ....

1026. $\dfrac{2}{9} \div \dfrac{4}{9} =$ ....

1027. $\dfrac{7}{11} \div \dfrac{6}{11} =$ ....

1028. $\dfrac{2}{10} \div \dfrac{5}{10} =$ ....

1029. $\dfrac{8}{11} \div \dfrac{5}{11} =$ ....

1030. $\dfrac{3}{7} \div \dfrac{1}{7} =$ ....

1031. $\dfrac{2}{8} \div \dfrac{1}{8} =$ ....

1032. $\dfrac{2}{10} \div \dfrac{2}{10} =$ ....

1033. $\dfrac{1}{8} \div \dfrac{2}{8} =$ ....

1034. $\dfrac{1}{7} \div \dfrac{5}{7} =$ ....

1035. $\dfrac{5}{11} \div \dfrac{6}{11} =$ ....

1036. $\dfrac{4}{9} \div \dfrac{2}{9} =$ ....

1037. $\dfrac{3}{7} \div \dfrac{2}{7} =$ ....

1038. $\dfrac{3}{10} \div \dfrac{5}{10} =$ ....

1039. $\dfrac{5}{9} \div \dfrac{5}{9} =$ ....

1040. $\dfrac{8}{11} \div \dfrac{8}{11} =$ ....

1041. $\dfrac{1}{11} \div \dfrac{5}{11} =$ ....

1042. $\dfrac{1}{7} \div \dfrac{3}{7} =$ ....

1043. $\dfrac{4}{9} \div \dfrac{4}{9} =$ ....

1044. $\dfrac{4}{10} \div \dfrac{7}{10} =$ ....

1045. $\dfrac{4}{8} \div \dfrac{6}{8} =$ ....

1046. $\dfrac{5}{10} \div \dfrac{5}{10} =$ ....

1047. $\dfrac{2}{11} \div \dfrac{7}{11} =$ ....

1048. $\dfrac{1}{7} \div \dfrac{4}{7} =$ ....

1049. $\dfrac{10}{11} \div \dfrac{5}{11} =$ ....

1050. $\dfrac{6}{9} \div \dfrac{2}{9} =$ ....

1051. $\dfrac{2}{8} \div \dfrac{4}{8} =$ ....

1052. $\dfrac{9}{10} \div \dfrac{7}{10} =$ ....

1053. $\dfrac{2}{10} \div \dfrac{7}{10} =$ ....

1054. $\dfrac{2}{11} \div \dfrac{8}{11} =$ ....

1055. $\dfrac{1}{8} \div \dfrac{1}{8} =$ ....

1056. $\dfrac{4}{9} \div \dfrac{3}{9} =$ ....

1057. $\dfrac{2}{3} \div \dfrac{2}{3} =$ ....

1058. $\dfrac{1}{2} \div \dfrac{2}{4} =$ ....

1059. $\dfrac{1}{2} \div \dfrac{1}{2} =$ ....

1060. $\dfrac{1}{6} \div \dfrac{2}{4} =$ ....

1061. $\dfrac{1}{3} \div \dfrac{1}{2} =$ ....

1062. $\dfrac{1}{2} \div \dfrac{1}{3} =$ ....

1063. $\dfrac{3}{6} \div \dfrac{4}{5} =$ ....

1064. $\dfrac{3}{4} \div \dfrac{2}{4} =$ ....

1065. $\dfrac{3}{5} \div \dfrac{1}{2} =$ ....

1066. $\dfrac{1}{4} \div \dfrac{4}{6} =$ ....

1067. $\dfrac{5}{6} \div \dfrac{1}{2} =$ ....

1068. $\dfrac{3}{5} \div \dfrac{2}{5} =$ ....

1069. $\dfrac{4}{5} \div \dfrac{1}{6} =$ ....

1070. $\dfrac{2}{4} \div \dfrac{2}{3} =$ ....

1071. $\dfrac{1}{2} \div \dfrac{2}{3} =$ ....

1072. $\dfrac{3}{6} \div \dfrac{2}{5} =$ ....

1073. $\dfrac{2}{3} \div \dfrac{1}{2} =$ ....

1074. $\dfrac{1}{2} \div \dfrac{1}{6} =$ ....

1075. $\dfrac{4}{5} \div \dfrac{1}{2} =$ ....

1076. $\dfrac{1}{2} \div \dfrac{3}{5} =$ ....

1077. $\dfrac{1}{6} \div \dfrac{1}{2} =$ ....

1078. $\dfrac{1}{5} \div \dfrac{4}{5} =$ ....

1079. $\dfrac{1}{2} \div \dfrac{5}{6} =$ ....

1080. $\dfrac{5}{6} \div \dfrac{4}{6} =$ ....

1081. $\dfrac{1}{3} \div \dfrac{3}{4} =$ ....

1082. $\dfrac{2}{5} \div \dfrac{1}{4} =$ ....

1083. $\dfrac{1}{5} \div \dfrac{4}{6} =$ ....

1084. $\dfrac{1}{4} \div \dfrac{1}{2} =$ ....

1085. $\dfrac{3}{5} \div \dfrac{4}{6} =$ ....

1086. $\dfrac{3}{4} \div \dfrac{4}{5} =$ ....

1087. $\dfrac{1}{3} \div \dfrac{1}{4} =$ ....

1088. $\dfrac{1}{3} \div \dfrac{3}{5} =$ ....

1089. $\dfrac{2}{5} \div \dfrac{1}{2} =$

1090. $\dfrac{3}{4} \div \dfrac{1}{6} =$

1091. $\dfrac{4}{6} \div \dfrac{1}{3} =$

1092. $\dfrac{1}{3} \div \dfrac{3}{6} =$

1093. $\dfrac{1}{5} \div \dfrac{1}{2} =$

1094. $\dfrac{1}{6} \div \dfrac{2}{3} =$

1095. $\dfrac{2}{3} \div \dfrac{5}{6} =$

1096. $\dfrac{3}{4} \div \dfrac{2}{5} =$

1097. $\dfrac{1}{2} \div \dfrac{1}{4} =$

1098. $\dfrac{2}{4} \div \dfrac{1}{2} =$

1099. $\dfrac{2}{3} \div \dfrac{1}{3} =$

1100. $\dfrac{2}{4} \div \dfrac{1}{5} =$

1101. $\dfrac{3}{4} \div \dfrac{1}{3} =$

1102. $\dfrac{1}{4} \div \dfrac{3}{4} =$

1103. $\dfrac{4}{5} \div \dfrac{2}{3} =$

1104. $\dfrac{4}{6} \div \dfrac{2}{3} =$

1105. $\dfrac{1}{6} \div \dfrac{1}{4} =$

1106. $\dfrac{2}{6} \div \dfrac{3}{6} =$

1107. $\dfrac{1}{3} \div \dfrac{2}{4} =$

1108. $\dfrac{2}{5} \div \dfrac{1}{6} =$

1109. $\dfrac{3}{6} \div \dfrac{1}{2} =$

1110. $\dfrac{3}{5} \div \dfrac{1}{3} =$

1111. $\dfrac{3}{6} \div \dfrac{1}{3} =$

1112. $\dfrac{1}{4} \div \dfrac{1}{5} =$

1113. $\dfrac{1}{5} \div \dfrac{1}{5} =$

1114. $\dfrac{3}{6} \div \dfrac{3}{6} =$

1115. $\dfrac{2}{5} \div \dfrac{1}{3} =$

1116. $\dfrac{3}{4} \div \dfrac{2}{6} =$

1117. $\dfrac{4}{5} \div \dfrac{2}{5} =$

1118. $\dfrac{1}{4} \div \dfrac{2}{3} =$

1119. $\dfrac{1}{2} \div \dfrac{3}{4} =$

1120. $\dfrac{1}{3} \div \dfrac{4}{5} =$

1121. $\dfrac{1}{4} \div \dfrac{1}{3} =$ ....

1122. $\dfrac{4}{6} \div \dfrac{1}{2} =$ ....

1123. $\dfrac{1}{3} \div \dfrac{1}{5} =$ ....

1124. $\dfrac{2}{5} \div \dfrac{2}{4} =$ ....

1125. $\dfrac{2}{3} \div \dfrac{4}{5} =$ ....

1126. $\dfrac{3}{4} \div \dfrac{1}{2} =$ ....

1127. $\dfrac{3}{6} \div \dfrac{1}{5} =$ ....

1128. $\dfrac{1}{4} \div \dfrac{2}{6} =$ ....

1129. $\dfrac{2}{3} \div \dfrac{2}{4} =$ ....

1130. $\dfrac{1}{5} \div \dfrac{3}{6} =$ ....

1131. $\dfrac{1}{2} \div \dfrac{1}{5} =$ ....

1132. $\dfrac{1}{2} \div \dfrac{2}{5} =$ ....

1133. $\dfrac{2}{3} \div \dfrac{1}{4} =$ ....

1134. $\dfrac{2}{4} \div \dfrac{1}{4} =$ ....

1135. $\dfrac{4}{5} \div \dfrac{2}{6} =$ ....

1136. $\dfrac{1}{4} \div \dfrac{1}{4} =$ ....

1137. $\dfrac{3}{5} \div \dfrac{1}{4} =$

1138. $\dfrac{1}{3} \div \dfrac{2}{3} =$

1139. $\dfrac{3}{4} \div \dfrac{5}{6} =$

1140. $\dfrac{5}{6} \div \dfrac{1}{5} =$

1141. $\dfrac{1}{3} \div \dfrac{2}{5} =$

1142. $\dfrac{1}{4} \div \dfrac{3}{5} =$

1143. $\dfrac{3}{6} \div \dfrac{4}{6} =$

1144. $\dfrac{1}{6} \div \dfrac{3}{4} =$

1145. $\dfrac{2}{4} \div \dfrac{4}{6} =$

1146. $\dfrac{1}{2} \div \dfrac{4}{5} =$

1147. $\dfrac{3}{5} \div \dfrac{3}{5} =$

1148. $\dfrac{1}{4} \div \dfrac{5}{6} =$

1149. $\dfrac{2}{6} \div \dfrac{1}{5} =$

1150. $\dfrac{4}{5} \div \dfrac{2}{4} =$

1151. $\dfrac{1}{2} \div \dfrac{2}{6} =$

1152. $\dfrac{1}{4} \div \dfrac{2}{5} =$

EXERCISES 5

FRACTIONS - CONVERTING

1153. $\dfrac{1}{3} = \dfrac{6}{}$

1154. $\dfrac{}{8} = \dfrac{7}{56}$

1155. $\dfrac{3}{} = \dfrac{30}{50}$

1156. $\dfrac{1}{6} = \dfrac{3}{}$

1157. $\dfrac{7}{} = \dfrac{63}{81}$

1158. $\dfrac{}{2} = \dfrac{8}{16}$

1159. $\dfrac{}{4} = \dfrac{4}{8}$

1160. $\dfrac{4}{} = \dfrac{12}{27}$

1161. $\dfrac{}{6} = \dfrac{30}{60}$

1162. $\dfrac{2}{3} = \dfrac{18}{}$

1163. $\dfrac{}{5} = \dfrac{24}{40}$

1164. $\dfrac{}{8} = \dfrac{8}{16}$

1165. $\dfrac{}{2} = \dfrac{6}{12}$

1166. $\dfrac{2}{} = \dfrac{6}{21}$

1167. $\dfrac{3}{} = \dfrac{15}{20}$

1168. $\dfrac{6}{9} = \dfrac{}{90}$

1169. $\dfrac{1}{5} = \dfrac{10}{}$

1170. $\dfrac{2}{4} = \dfrac{}{16}$

1171. $\dfrac{7}{8} = \dfrac{28}{}$

1172. $\dfrac{3}{6} = \dfrac{}{48}$

1173. $\dfrac{4}{7} = \dfrac{8}{}$

1174. $\dfrac{1}{2} = \dfrac{9}{}$

1175. $\dfrac{}{3} = \dfrac{2}{6}$

1176. $\dfrac{2}{} = \dfrac{14}{21}$

1177. $\dfrac{8}{} = \dfrac{80}{90}$

1178. $\dfrac{4}{7} = \dfrac{36}{}$

1179. $\dfrac{2}{5} = \dfrac{}{20}$

1180. $\dfrac{}{6} = \dfrac{28}{42}$

1181. $\dfrac{1}{2} = \dfrac{}{10}$

1182. $\dfrac{2}{8} = \dfrac{}{16}$

1183. $\dfrac{3}{} = \dfrac{18}{24}$

1184. $\dfrac{7}{9} = \dfrac{}{63}$

1185. $\dfrac{4}{} = \dfrac{20}{30}$

1186. $\dfrac{7}{8} = \dfrac{70}{}$

1187. $\dfrac{1}{7} = \dfrac{}{56}$

1188. $\dfrac{}{7} = \dfrac{28}{49}$

1189. $\dfrac{2}{} = \dfrac{12}{30}$

1190. $\dfrac{1}{4} = \dfrac{10}{}$

1191. $\dfrac{1}{2} = \dfrac{7}{}$

1192. $\dfrac{6}{} = \dfrac{36}{48}$

1193. $\dfrac{5}{6} = \dfrac{}{60}$

1194. $\dfrac{7}{9} = \dfrac{}{54}$

1195. $\dfrac{4}{} = \dfrac{40}{90}$

1196. $\dfrac{3}{4} = \dfrac{6}{}$

1197. $\dfrac{}{7} = \dfrac{10}{70}$

1198. $\dfrac{1}{2} = \dfrac{}{4}$

1199. $\dfrac{2}{} = \dfrac{14}{42}$

1200. $\dfrac{3}{5} = \dfrac{21}{}$

1201. $\dfrac{6}{} = \dfrac{54}{72}$

1202. $\dfrac{1}{8} = \dfrac{}{72}$

1203. $\dfrac{1}{3} = \dfrac{}{24}$

1204. $\dfrac{}{9} = \dfrac{48}{54}$

1205. $\dfrac{2}{7} = \dfrac{}{35}$

1206. $\dfrac{2}{6} = \dfrac{8}{}$

1207. $\dfrac{1}{} = \dfrac{6}{24}$

1208. $\dfrac{1}{4} = \dfrac{9}{}$

1209. $\dfrac{}{6} = \dfrac{16}{24}$

1210. $\dfrac{1}{3} = \dfrac{}{9}$

1211. $\dfrac{3}{} = \dfrac{27}{45}$

1212. $\dfrac{4}{9} = \dfrac{}{72}$

1213. $\dfrac{}{7} = \dfrac{30}{42}$

1214. $\dfrac{}{9} = \dfrac{24}{36}$

1215. $\dfrac{4}{} = \dfrac{36}{54}$

1216. $\dfrac{2}{} = \dfrac{16}{32}$

1217. $\dfrac{}{3} = \dfrac{12}{18}$

1218. $\dfrac{1}{2} = \dfrac{4}{}$

1219. $\dfrac{2}{} = \dfrac{6}{24}$

1220. $\dfrac{}{7} = \dfrac{10}{14}$

1221. $\dfrac{1}{8} = \dfrac{4}{}$

1222. $\dfrac{1}{} = \dfrac{10}{20}$

1223. $\dfrac{5}{} = \dfrac{20}{36}$

1224. $\dfrac{3}{} = \dfrac{21}{42}$

1225. $\dfrac{1}{3} = \dfrac{5}{}$

1226. $\dfrac{2}{4} = \dfrac{}{36}$

1227. $\dfrac{}{7} = \dfrac{30}{35}$

1228. $\dfrac{}{9} = \dfrac{6}{18}$

1229. $\dfrac{}{4} = \dfrac{24}{32}$

1230. $\dfrac{1}{} = \dfrac{5}{30}$

1231. $\dfrac{7}{8} = \dfrac{35}{}$

1232. $\dfrac{1}{5} = \dfrac{9}{}$

1233. $\dfrac{}{6} = \dfrac{2}{12}$

1234. $\dfrac{1}{7} = \dfrac{5}{}$

1235. $\dfrac{6}{9} = \dfrac{48}{}$

1236. $\dfrac{2}{4} = \dfrac{14}{}$

1237. $\dfrac{1}{2} = \dfrac{}{6} = \dfrac{2}{}$

1238. $\dfrac{3}{4} = \dfrac{}{16} = \dfrac{}{8}$

1239. $\dfrac{2}{3} = \dfrac{}{9} = \dfrac{}{12}$

1240. $\dfrac{1}{5} = \dfrac{}{50} = \dfrac{}{30}$

1241. $\dfrac{3}{5} = \dfrac{}{25} = \dfrac{}{30}$

1242. $\dfrac{2}{4} = \dfrac{8}{} = \dfrac{18}{}$

1243. $\dfrac{2}{3} = \dfrac{}{24} = \dfrac{6}{}$

1244. $\dfrac{1}{2} = \dfrac{}{14} = \dfrac{}{4}$

1245. $\dfrac{1}{4} = \dfrac{}{36} = \dfrac{}{16}$

1246. $\dfrac{4}{5} = \dfrac{16}{} = \dfrac{}{40}$

1247. $\dfrac{2}{3} = \dfrac{}{24} = \dfrac{}{30}$

1248. $\dfrac{2}{3} = \dfrac{}{9} = \dfrac{14}{}$

1249. $\dfrac{2}{5} = \dfrac{6}{} = \dfrac{20}{}$

1250. $\dfrac{2}{4} = \dfrac{}{16} = \dfrac{}{12}$

1251. $\dfrac{1}{2} = \dfrac{}{18} = \dfrac{}{4}$

1252. $\dfrac{1}{2} = \dfrac{9}{} = \dfrac{}{6}$

1253. $\dfrac{4}{5} = \dfrac{32}{} = \dfrac{}{25}$

1254. $\dfrac{1}{3} = \dfrac{8}{} = \dfrac{}{9}$

1255. $\dfrac{3}{4} = \dfrac{}{8} = \dfrac{15}{}$

1256. $\dfrac{2}{3} = \dfrac{20}{} = \dfrac{8}{}$

1257. $\dfrac{4}{5} = \dfrac{}{40} = \dfrac{8}{}$

1258. $\dfrac{1}{2} = \dfrac{}{20} = \dfrac{}{16}$

1259. $\dfrac{1}{4} = \dfrac{5}{} = \dfrac{}{24}$

1260. $\dfrac{1}{2} = \dfrac{}{10} = \dfrac{10}{}$

1261. $\dfrac{4}{5} = \dfrac{40}{} = \dfrac{}{20}$

1262. $\dfrac{2}{4} = \dfrac{}{24} = \dfrac{}{20}$

1263. $\dfrac{1}{3} = \dfrac{4}{} = \dfrac{3}{}$

1264. $\dfrac{1}{3} = \dfrac{}{15} = \dfrac{3}{}$

1265. $\dfrac{2}{4} = \dfrac{4}{} = \dfrac{}{12}$

1266. $\dfrac{4}{5} = \dfrac{36}{} = \dfrac{16}{}$

1267. $\dfrac{3}{5} = \dfrac{}{30} = \dfrac{12}{}$

1268. $\dfrac{1}{2} = \dfrac{}{12} = \dfrac{7}{}$

1269. $\dfrac{2}{4} = \dfrac{6}{} = \dfrac{10}{}$

1270. $\dfrac{2}{3} = \dfrac{}{27} = \dfrac{10}{}$

1271. $\dfrac{3}{5} = \dfrac{12}{} = \dfrac{}{15}$

1272. $\dfrac{1}{3} = \dfrac{}{21} = \dfrac{5}{}$

1273. $\dfrac{1}{4} = \dfrac{6}{} = \dfrac{}{36}$

1274. $\dfrac{1}{2} = \dfrac{9}{} = \dfrac{10}{}$

1275. $\dfrac{1}{3} = \dfrac{}{9} = \dfrac{9}{}$

1276. $\dfrac{4}{5} = \dfrac{}{35} = \dfrac{}{20}$

1277. $\dfrac{1}{4} = \dfrac{}{36} = \dfrac{}{24}$

1278. $\dfrac{1}{2} = \dfrac{3}{} = \dfrac{5}{}$

1279. $\dfrac{2}{3} = \dfrac{}{27} = \dfrac{}{21}$

1280. $\dfrac{4}{5} = \dfrac{}{15} = \dfrac{40}{}$

1281. $\dfrac{1}{4} = \dfrac{}{8} = \dfrac{6}{}$

1282. $\dfrac{1}{2} = \dfrac{}{20} = \dfrac{3}{}$

1283. $\dfrac{2}{4} = \dfrac{12}{} = \dfrac{20}{}$

1284. $\dfrac{1}{2} = \dfrac{}{6} = \dfrac{10}{}$

1285. $\dfrac{1}{5} = \dfrac{}{25} = \dfrac{}{40}$

1286. $\dfrac{2}{3} = \dfrac{18}{} = \dfrac{20}{}$

1287. $\dfrac{2}{4} = \dfrac{}{32} = \dfrac{20}{}$

1288. $\dfrac{1}{5} = \dfrac{2}{} = \dfrac{}{40}$

1289. $\dfrac{1}{3} = \dfrac{}{30} = \dfrac{}{15}$

1290. $\dfrac{1}{2} = \dfrac{3}{} = \dfrac{4}{}$

1291. $\dfrac{1}{2} = \dfrac{2}{} = \dfrac{3}{}$

1292. $\dfrac{3}{5} = \dfrac{9}{} = \dfrac{30}{}$

1293. $\dfrac{1}{3} = \dfrac{}{24} = \dfrac{9}{}$

1294. $\dfrac{3}{4} = \dfrac{12}{} = \dfrac{}{12}$

1295. $\dfrac{1}{2} = \dfrac{4}{} = \dfrac{}{12}$

1296. $\dfrac{3}{5} = \dfrac{}{15} = \dfrac{}{45}$

1297. $\dfrac{1}{3} = \dfrac{}{15} = \dfrac{}{24}$

1298. $\dfrac{3}{4} = \dfrac{9}{} = \dfrac{}{20}$

1299. $\dfrac{1}{3} = \dfrac{10}{} = \dfrac{}{18}$

1300. $\dfrac{3}{4} = \dfrac{21}{} = \dfrac{27}{}$

1301. $\dfrac{4}{5} = \dfrac{24}{} = \dfrac{}{25}$

1302. $\dfrac{1}{2} = \dfrac{}{4} = \dfrac{8}{}$

1303. $\dfrac{2}{3} = \dfrac{}{21} = \dfrac{}{27}$

1304. $\dfrac{3}{5} = \dfrac{18}{} = \dfrac{}{10}$

1305. $\dfrac{1}{2} = \dfrac{7}{} = \dfrac{9}{}$

1306. $\dfrac{3}{4} = \dfrac{24}{} = \dfrac{}{36}$

1307. $\dfrac{1}{2} = \dfrac{8}{} = \dfrac{9}{}$

1308. $\dfrac{1}{3} = \dfrac{}{18} = \dfrac{}{27}$

1309. $\dfrac{3}{5} = \dfrac{}{10} = \dfrac{18}{}$

1310. $\dfrac{2}{4} = \dfrac{}{16} = \dfrac{}{20}$

1311. $\dfrac{1}{2} = \dfrac{}{14} = \dfrac{}{6}$

1312. $\dfrac{2}{5} = \dfrac{12}{} = \dfrac{8}{}$

1313. $\dfrac{3}{4} = \dfrac{21}{} = \dfrac{}{16}$

1314. $\dfrac{1}{2} = \dfrac{}{16} = \dfrac{}{10}$

1315. $\dfrac{3}{5} = \dfrac{}{40} = \dfrac{21}{}$

1316. $\dfrac{2}{4} = \dfrac{}{12} = \dfrac{12}{}$

1317. $\dfrac{1}{2} = \dfrac{5}{} = \dfrac{}{18}$

1318. $\dfrac{2}{5} = \dfrac{10}{} = \dfrac{}{15}$

1319. $\dfrac{1}{3} = \dfrac{6}{} = \dfrac{5}{}$

1320. $\dfrac{3}{4} = \dfrac{27}{} = \dfrac{15}{}$

1321. $\dfrac{3}{5} = \dfrac{18}{} = \dfrac{}{25} = \dfrac{}{50}$

1322. $\dfrac{2}{3} = \dfrac{}{30} = \dfrac{16}{} = \dfrac{}{15}$

1323. $\dfrac{1}{2} = \dfrac{4}{} = \dfrac{6}{} = \dfrac{5}{}$

1324. $\dfrac{4}{5} = \dfrac{24}{} = \dfrac{}{20} = \dfrac{8}{}$

1325. $\dfrac{1}{3} = \dfrac{4}{} = \dfrac{}{30} = \dfrac{}{27}$

1326. $\dfrac{3}{4} = \dfrac{12}{} = \dfrac{}{32} = \dfrac{}{20}$

1327. $\dfrac{1}{2} = \dfrac{}{6} = \dfrac{}{8} = \dfrac{}{4}$

1328. $\dfrac{1}{3} = \dfrac{}{30} = \dfrac{9}{} = \dfrac{6}{}$

1329. $\dfrac{1}{4} = \dfrac{}{16} = \dfrac{10}{} = \dfrac{3}{}$

1330. $\dfrac{1}{5} = \dfrac{4}{} = \dfrac{}{30} = \dfrac{}{10}$

1331. $\dfrac{1}{2} = \dfrac{9}{} = \dfrac{}{12} = \dfrac{}{18}$

1332. $\dfrac{1}{4} = \dfrac{}{24} = \dfrac{8}{} = \dfrac{7}{}$

1333. $\dfrac{2}{3} = \dfrac{}{18} = \dfrac{}{6} = \dfrac{12}{}$

1334. $\dfrac{1}{2} = \dfrac{7}{} = \dfrac{}{18} = \dfrac{}{6}$

1335. $\dfrac{2}{5} = \dfrac{}{15} = \dfrac{20}{} = \dfrac{8}{}$

1336. $\dfrac{1}{3} = \dfrac{}{9} = \dfrac{}{27} = \dfrac{}{30}$

1337. $\dfrac{1}{5} = \dfrac{4}{} = \dfrac{9}{} = \dfrac{}{15}$

1338. $\dfrac{1}{4} = \dfrac{9}{} = \dfrac{}{8} = \dfrac{5}{}$

1339. $\dfrac{1}{2} = \dfrac{}{10} = \dfrac{2}{} = \dfrac{}{12}$

1340. $\dfrac{4}{5} = \dfrac{}{30} = \dfrac{20}{} = \dfrac{}{10}$

1341. $\dfrac{1}{2} = \dfrac{}{20} = \dfrac{5}{} = \dfrac{}{14}$

1342. $\dfrac{1}{3} = \dfrac{9}{} = \dfrac{}{9} = \dfrac{9}{}$

1343. $\dfrac{2}{4} = \dfrac{}{20} = \dfrac{}{8} = \dfrac{}{28}$

1344. $\dfrac{2}{3} = \dfrac{8}{} = \dfrac{}{15} = \dfrac{14}{}$

1345. $\dfrac{4}{5} = \dfrac{}{40} = \dfrac{16}{} = \dfrac{}{40}$

1346. $\dfrac{3}{4} = \dfrac{24}{} = \dfrac{18}{} = \dfrac{6}{}$

1347. $\dfrac{1}{2} = \dfrac{}{18} = \dfrac{}{10} = \dfrac{4}{}$

1348. $\dfrac{2}{5} = \dfrac{}{20} = \dfrac{}{15} = \dfrac{}{40}$

1349. $\dfrac{1}{2} = \dfrac{}{16} = \dfrac{9}{} = \dfrac{}{6}$

1350. $\dfrac{2}{3} = \dfrac{4}{} = \dfrac{16}{} = \dfrac{}{9}$

1351. $\dfrac{1}{4} = \dfrac{}{40} = \dfrac{}{32} = \dfrac{6}{}$

1352. $\dfrac{2}{3} = \dfrac{14}{} = \dfrac{}{27} = \dfrac{}{18}$

1353. $\dfrac{3}{4} = \dfrac{9}{} = \dfrac{6}{} = \dfrac{12}{}$

1354. $\dfrac{1}{2} = \dfrac{6}{} = \dfrac{9}{} = \dfrac{7}{}$

1355. $\dfrac{2}{5} = \dfrac{}{35} = \dfrac{}{40} = \dfrac{}{15}$

1356. $\dfrac{1}{5} = \dfrac{}{25} = \dfrac{2}{} = \dfrac{}{40}$

1357. $\dfrac{2}{3} = \dfrac{}{15} = \dfrac{}{30} = \dfrac{10}{}$

1358. $\dfrac{2}{4} = \dfrac{}{28} = \dfrac{}{32} = \dfrac{}{12}$

1359. $\dfrac{1}{2} = \dfrac{}{20} = \dfrac{}{4} = \dfrac{5}{}$

1360. $\dfrac{2}{3} = \dfrac{16}{} = \dfrac{8}{} = \dfrac{10}{}$

1361. $\dfrac{3}{5} = \dfrac{}{25} = \dfrac{12}{} = \dfrac{}{40}$

1362. $\dfrac{2}{4} = \dfrac{}{12} = \dfrac{}{8} = \dfrac{}{20}$

1363. $\dfrac{1}{2} = \dfrac{}{18} = \dfrac{}{8} = \dfrac{}{20}$

1364. $\dfrac{1}{4} = \dfrac{}{24} = \dfrac{10}{} = \dfrac{6}{}$

1365. $\dfrac{2}{3} = \dfrac{}{21} = \dfrac{}{30} = \dfrac{12}{}$

1366. $\dfrac{1}{2} = \dfrac{5}{} = \dfrac{}{4} = \dfrac{5}{}$

1367. $\dfrac{1}{5} = \dfrac{}{20} = \dfrac{7}{} = \dfrac{2}{}$

1368. $\dfrac{1}{4} = \dfrac{8}{} = \dfrac{}{40} = \dfrac{3}{}$

1369. $\dfrac{3}{5} = \dfrac{}{40} = \dfrac{21}{} = \dfrac{9}{}$

1370. $\dfrac{2}{3} = \dfrac{}{24} = \dfrac{}{21} = \dfrac{}{12}$

1371. $\dfrac{1}{2} = \dfrac{}{10} = \dfrac{}{6} = \dfrac{}{8}$

1372. $\dfrac{3}{4} = \dfrac{}{8} = \dfrac{}{16} = \dfrac{24}{}$

1373. $\dfrac{1}{3} = \dfrac{}{27} = \dfrac{3}{} = \dfrac{7}{}$

1374. $\dfrac{4}{5} = \dfrac{}{30} = \dfrac{8}{} = \dfrac{}{40}$

1375. $\dfrac{1}{2} = \dfrac{}{6} = \dfrac{}{4} = \dfrac{}{12}$

1376. $\dfrac{1}{3} = \dfrac{}{30} = \dfrac{}{18} = \dfrac{10}{}$

1377. $\dfrac{1}{4} = \dfrac{8}{} = \dfrac{}{36} = \dfrac{2}{}$

1378. $\dfrac{2}{5} = \dfrac{6}{} = \dfrac{16}{} = \dfrac{14}{}$

1379. $\dfrac{2}{3} = \dfrac{10}{} = \dfrac{}{6} = \dfrac{}{12}$

1380. $\dfrac{1}{2} = \dfrac{3}{} = \dfrac{7}{} = \dfrac{}{6}$

1381. $\dfrac{1}{5} = \dfrac{}{15} = \dfrac{}{45} = \dfrac{8}{}$

1382. $\dfrac{3}{4} = \dfrac{}{8} = \dfrac{18}{} = \dfrac{15}{}$

1383. $\dfrac{1}{3} = \dfrac{9}{} = \dfrac{}{15} = \dfrac{2}{}$

1384. $\dfrac{1}{4} = \dfrac{5}{} = \dfrac{6}{} = \dfrac{}{12}$

1385. $\dfrac{1}{2} = \dfrac{}{16} = \dfrac{2}{} = \dfrac{}{20}$

1386. $\dfrac{2}{5} = \dfrac{16}{} = \dfrac{4}{} = \dfrac{}{20}$

1387. $\dfrac{1}{2} = \dfrac{}{16} = \dfrac{}{14} = \dfrac{8}{}$

1388. $\dfrac{2}{4} = \dfrac{}{40} = \dfrac{}{20} = \dfrac{4}{}$

1389. $\dfrac{2}{5} = \dfrac{}{35} = \dfrac{}{30} = \dfrac{16}{}$

1390. $\dfrac{1}{3} = \dfrac{}{12} = \dfrac{5}{} = \dfrac{8}{}$

1391. $\dfrac{1}{2} = \dfrac{6}{} = \dfrac{5}{} = \dfrac{}{8}$

1392. $\dfrac{2}{4} = \dfrac{6}{} = \dfrac{4}{} = \dfrac{}{12}$

1393. $\dfrac{2}{3} = \dfrac{14}{} = \dfrac{}{6} = \dfrac{}{9}$

1394. $\dfrac{2}{5} = \dfrac{18}{} = \dfrac{}{25} = \dfrac{}{20}$

1395. $\dfrac{1}{4} = \dfrac{9}{} = \dfrac{}{20} = \dfrac{7}{}$

1396. $\dfrac{4}{5} = \dfrac{}{15} = \dfrac{40}{} = \dfrac{28}{}$

1397. $\dfrac{1}{3} = \dfrac{5}{} = \dfrac{}{30} = \dfrac{4}{}$

1398. $\dfrac{3}{4} = \dfrac{}{32} = \dfrac{15}{} = \dfrac{}{32}$

1399. $\dfrac{2}{3} = \dfrac{8}{} = \dfrac{}{24} = \dfrac{}{27}$

1400. $\dfrac{4}{5} = \dfrac{40}{} = \dfrac{36}{} = \dfrac{}{40}$

1401. $\dfrac{1}{2} = \dfrac{}{8} = \dfrac{9}{} = \dfrac{}{20}$

1402. $\dfrac{4}{5} = \dfrac{}{35} = \dfrac{}{30} = \dfrac{}{15}$

1403. $\dfrac{1}{3} = \dfrac{}{21} = \dfrac{6}{} = \dfrac{}{27}$

1404. $\dfrac{1}{2} = \dfrac{6}{} = \dfrac{}{4} = \dfrac{6}{}$